THE
Revenge
Encyclopedia

THE
Revenge Encyclopedia

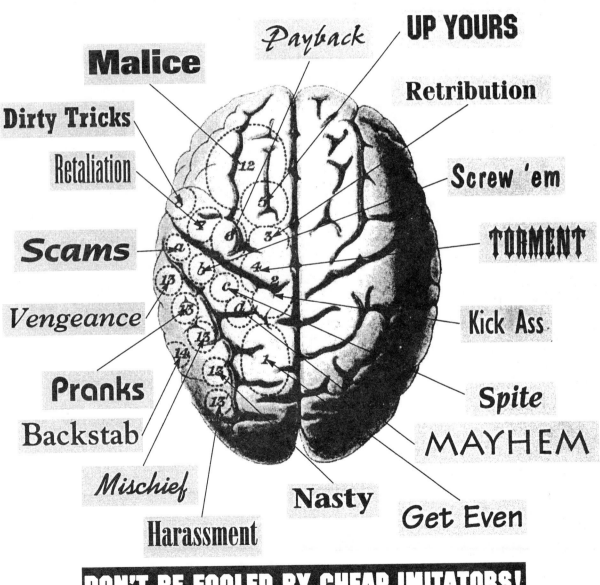

Payback UP YOURS

Malice Retribution

Dirty Tricks

Retaliation Screw 'em

Scams TORMENT

Vengeance Kick Ass

Pranks Spite

Backstab MAYHEM

Mischief Nasty Get Even

Harassment

PALADIN PRESS • BOULDER, COLORADO

The Revenge Encyclopedia

Copyright © 1995 by Paladin Press

ISBN 0-87364-851-X
Printed in the United States of America

Published by Paladin Press, a division of
Paladin Enterprises, Inc.
Gunbarrel Tech Center
7077 Winchester Circle
Boulder, Colorado 80301 USA
+1.303.443.7250

Direct inquiries and/or orders to the above address.

Visit our Web site at www.paladin-press.com

CONTENTS

WARNING

The schemes, tricks, scams, stunts, cons, and scenarios presented here are for *information and amusement purposes only*. The publisher of this book does not expect that anyone who reads this book would actually ever do any of the things described here. It is not intended to instruct or persuade anyone to commit any unpleasant or illegal acts.

PREFACE

The Revenge Encyclopedia is the most authoritative book on revenge available anywhere. It contains almost 1,000 tricks to suit every occasion and evildoer. The tricks are arranged alphabetically and were designed to be adapted to your special needs. So use your imagination when applying them.

Revenge is a time-honored method of serving notice to bullies and bad guys that they are treading on thin ice when they mess with you or yours. But, though presented here in a light-hearted manner, revenge is not a subject to be taken lightly. While it is true that revenge is not rocket science, administered correctly, it is a science—and an art. Teaching you the proper techniques of revengemanship is the purpose of this book.

If you have read any of Paladin's other revenge books, you already know how to use this book. And even if you haven't, you probably think you know. The bad guy does something to you, and you get even with him. What could be simpler? But revenge is not like a schoolyard fight where you get hit and then get up and punch the bully in the nose. The end result is the same: the bully gets his due and he leaves you alone from then on. But when performing the techiques described in this book, you don't want anyone to know that you are responsible for the mark's sudden bad fortune. So a few rules are in order to ensure success and anonymity.

First, the punishment should fit the crime. Avenging a wrong is not about taking advantage of someone or becoming a bully yourself.

Second, as the old Sicilian proverb states: Revenge is a dish best served cold. Make sure that you allow enough time to pass between when the bully strikes you and when you retaliate to not call attention to you. The time you spend waiting and cooling off allows you to get all the details worked out.

Third, never leave a paper trail. Pay cash for everything you'll be using, never credit cards or checks. Don't use your home or work phone, or those of close friends or family, to make phone calls related to your retribution. Don't use your own name, address, or Social Security number.

Fourth, buy all your supplies from out of town merchants. Don't have any materials sent to your home or office.

Fifth, silence is golden. Never tell anyone who doesn't have a need to know about your planned or executed revenge.

Sixth, *never* admit anything. Chances are, if you've followed the above rules, they can't prove anything anyway.

Finally, we don't expect you to actually go out and do any of these tricks. This book is intended for *entertainment purposes only.*

ABORTION

- Send for abortion advice in the name of your newly—happily—pregnant target (or her partner).
- If you want to get back at an ex-boyfriend, write his parents a letter saying that you are his new girlfriend, you are pregnant, and their son keeps pressuring you to have an abortion.
- If you want to get back at an ex-girlfriend, write a letter to her parents and say she's pregnant and has been bugging you for money to help her pay for an abortion.
- If you're pro-choice, next time there is an antiabortion demonstration, take a photo of each demonstrator. Give each photo to a pro-choice person who agrees to make a small monetary donation to the local pro-choice cause in the photo subject's name and to contact that pro-lifer to offer counseling, humor, advice, old leftovers . . .

ACCIDENTS

- If you see a parked car that's been dented, and the offending driver has left his name and address in a note on the windshield, replace it with a note bearing your mark's name, address, and phone number.

ADDITIVES

- Yohimbine hydrochloride, a veterinary aphrodisiac, can be obtained from a pharmaceutical supply house. Find a way to slip a dose to your mark, your mark's dog, her mother, her horse . . .
- Add soaps or detergents to your target's foods or drinks, or generously coat his drinking vessels or utensils with liquid dishwashing detergent and let them dry. Then if you can find a key, lock all of his bathroom doors.
- The leaves, flowers, and bark of the senna plant are contained in some teas. Dried, these additives are a powerful laxative. Tea and "cramplets" anyone?
- *Cascara segrada* is an additive made from the dried root of a U.S.West Coast thorny shrub. When consumed, it causes explosive diarrhea in 10 to 15 minutes. Could add a little spice to a traffic jam. *Warning*: This one should *not* be used on senior citizens; it could cause them serious health problems.
- Syrup of ipecac, a common purgative, is available at any drugstore. One tablespoon added to a sweet, heavy drink that will hide the taste and consistency of the syrup will cause violent projectile vomiting about 15 minutes after it's consumed.
- Employ bottlecappers used by home brewers to re-cap your mark's bottles after you have added something lively to his beer.

- Sulfuric acid will corrode gutters, eaves, and downspouts.
- Salt will ruin the surface of a floor or will kill grass and other plants.
- Copper salts will dissolve rubber.
- Soap added to a fountain will create enormous amounts of foam.
- Light, coarse materials such as resin added to automotive fuel or metal filings dumped in the gears of machinery will create damage by friction.
- Apply some Visible Detection Paste (available at most police supply shops) to your mark's doorknobs, armrests, chairs, toilet seats. When it contacts human skin, it turns the contact areas bright purple and is tough to wash off.
- Replace the contents of your target's hemorrhoid cream with Vicks Vapo Rub.

ADVERTISING

- For a payback with staying power, take out a yellow pages ad in your mark's behalf under "Escort Services." Don't forget to hint at special services that are available and mention that it's a 24-hour service.
- Print up some "business cards" on your target's behalf and put them up on bulletin boards around town. Your target could offer any number of services: colonic irrigation (senior discounts), strip-o-grams, black magic, voodoo . . .
- Print up legitimate business cards for your mark, listing his name and actual job, place of work, and business phone. Then go to a few sleazy bars, make friends with some prostitutes, tramps, and boring old farts and give them "your" card, insisting that they call you tomorrow. Offer to lend them money, buy them dinner, or provide a place to stay.

AIR CONDITIONER

- Sabotage your mark's window air conditioning unit by sticking a wad of chewed gum up the condensation drain tube. With luck your mark won't notice the overflow until his floor tiles lift off because of the flooding moisture.

AIRLINES

- To get even with an airline for losing or misdirecting your luggage and to make a little money in the process, find an airport that doesn't employ a baggage clerk to collect baggage claim checks. Give a friend your baggage claim checks and have him claim your luggage for you and return the baggage claim checks to you. Then you go to claim your baggage and, after waiting a while for your bags to arrive, ask a clerk for assistance, showing them your claim checks as proof of missing luggage. When your luggage isn't found, demand satisfaction. You will be required to fill out some forms, and the airline will put a tracer on your luggage. When it fails to be located, you should receive a handsome settlement from the irresponsible airline.
- Leave legitimate-looking hijack plans, bomb diagrams, or terrorist attack scenarios in airport bars and rest rooms. They will make police and security personnel jump into action. Related flight delays and increased security checks will tick off passengers, who will take their anger out on the airlines and the airport. If some group has been particularly bothersome to you, find a way to connect its name to the "plans."
- To ward off religious panhandlers in

airports, do what the group FROGIE (Fellowship to Resist Organized Groups Involved in Exploitation) does. They arm themselves with small metal clickers shaped like frogs, and, when they are accosted by someone bent on their conversion, they haul out the clicker and click it in their intruders' faces until they give up and go on to save some other poor soul.

- If you're so equipped, and you are followed out of the airport by a persistent organized beggar, unzip your pants and urinate on the religious nut. It's guaranteed to dampen his spirit.
- Held over in an airport for an unusually long time while the plane's engine is being overhauled? Reduce your boredom by using the white paging telephones and asking the unsuspecting airline operators to page various nonexistent friends like Dr. Harry P. Ness, Rocky Piles, Philip Mabutt, Seymour Heinie, and so on. The secret is to spell, not say, the names to the operator.

AIR POLLUTERS

- Have a neighbor who burns just about everything in his fireplace, never giving a thought to the odoriferous smoke that pours out of his chimney and into the lungs of innocent passersby? Next time the jerk goes on vacation, get up on his roof and pour some soft tar down his chimney stack. The next time he lights a fire in his fireplace, the heat will ignite the soft tar coating in the chimney.

AIR TRAVELERS

- If you know the travel agent your mark uses, or the airline she is about to travel on, call and cancel her reservations. This works especially well during busy holiday seasons when new reservations will likely be impossible to make.
- If you can do it unnoticed, slip some drugs, a switchblade knife, or some pistol ammunition into your mark's pocket or purse just before he goes through the airport metal detector.
- If your target has "super saver" plane reservations (the kind that allows no changes in flight date and does not give refunds), cancel them. Your mark won't find out they've been canceled until he gets to the airport.
- If you have access to your target's briefcase or other carryon luggage, get a roll of assay lead (soft, thin sheets that can be cut easily with scissors) and cut silhouettes of pistols, trench knives, and the like. Stick the cutouts between the pages of some sleazy magazine and put it in the carryon. When the luggage goes through the metal detector, the guards will stop your mark to check out the suspicious items. When they find the cutouts, they'll think your mark is playing games with them . . . something they really don't take kindly to.
- After your mark checks in for her flight, switch the labels on her luggage and send her stuff on a holiday of its own.
- If your mark is the least bit afraid of flying, wait until you're airborne, then ask the flight attendant to deliver a message to the mark for you. Hand the attendant a sealed envelope, point out your mark, saying he's your uncle and what you are asking her to deliver is an unexpected birthday surprise. Have the note say something fun like, "Please be discreet. If you have any flying experience, come to the front of the airplane; the pilot's dead."

ANATOMY

- If your mark is a prude, arrange the fruits and vegetables in her refrigerator to resemble anatomical parts. Kiwi fruit and bananas make a nice showing.
- Cut a Nerf football half and then mount each half lengthwise on a small wooden panel a tad larger than the football halves. Glue a handle to the other side of the panel. Next, paint each half flesh-colored and take an old pair of pants, cut two inches down from the waistband, and glue them to the board just at the bottom of the "ass." Glue a shirttail at the top to complete the project. To activate this artificial moon, just hold the handle and press the cheek side firmly against your car, bus, van, or train window.

ANIMALS

- When you know your mark will be away on a several-day business trip, pick up a small dead animal from the road (birds, turtles, and prairie dogs are usually easy to get your hands on), find the mark's car in the train or airport parking lot, find a way to get into the car, and stuff the dead animal into the glove compartment. (A dead prairie dog is a vengeful man's [or woman's] best friend.)
- If you are bothered by a loose, barking, biting dog, carry a water gun filled with lemon juice, onion juice, or Tabasco Sauce when you know you will be going near the dog's house. When it attacks, you shoot it in the eyes with the juice. It will think twice (that is, if dogs really do think) before coming after you again.
- If your neighbor's dog constantly barks and howls, call the local SPCA and tell them that your neighbor mistreats the dog. Hold your phone up to an open door so the SPCA official can hear firsthand the dog's reaction to being abused.
- Type up an anonymous note saying exactly what you think of your target and attach it to his pet's collar.
- Entice cats into your target's garden with a liberal sprinkling of oriental fish sauce or encourage dogs to dig up the flower beds by seeding them with chunks of meat.
- If your neighbor's dog barks all day and stops only when its owners come home, get a dog whistle and use it as soon as they get home so they can have a taste of what you have to go through all day. The sound, inaudible to humans, will have the dog howling in a jiffy.
- If your target is a farmer, wait till the family leaves home for a little while, then march a few cows, sheep, and pigs into the house and shut them in. Leave water for them, especially if they're not likely to be discovered in short order.
- Put a live snake in your mark's clothes hamper or in her car or desk drawer.
- If your target has riding horses, put a few good-sized burs in the underside of the saddle blanket. Next time your target mounts, the horse will see that he dismounts just as quickly.
- Crows hate owls, so . . . if you can get up there, put a stuffed or plastic owl on your target's house where it is visible from the air but not the ground. Crows are persistent, raucous, and will eat and dump wherever they happen to be.
- Skunks love eggs and cheese. Why not make your mark a little omelet and leave it on the floor of his car? Leave the car door open and wait for the skunks to arrive. Then for a little added excitement, invite your mark's dog to join them for dinner.

- Salt is the condiment porcupines think is "to die for." If your mark lives in an area that has porcupines, saturate any wooden thing he owns with salt. The pokey little guys will take care of the rest.
- Pick up all of the dead animals in your neighborhood (rats, cats, squirrels, bunnies, birds), put them in bags, and keep them in your freezer until you have 20 to 30 of them. They make wonderful lawn ornaments for some deserving neighbor. Or place them on lawn furniture or near the patio or pool in sexually explicit positions just before your mark has a garden party.
- Collect some dog urine in a pan, and allow it to dry. Reconstitute it with alcohol and then place it in a small bottle like a nasal spray container. Spray the contents on the pant legs or hemline of your mark's clothing. The alcohol dries quickly and leaves the residue of dog urine. Other dogs that get close will try to mark the mark as their own territory.

ANSWERING MACHINES

- Record the target's answering machine greeting and play it back as a message into his system. Do this several times a day for about a week. He will think his machine is not operating properly.
- When you reach a number that has been disconnected, is out of order, or is not a working number, record that message on your portable tape recorder and play back as the message on your answering machine. This will stop bill collectors, phone solicitors, and ex-spouses from calling and leaving unwanted messages. Inform anyone you wish to take calls from to wait for the beep and leave a message.
- Change the outgoing message on your mark's office answering machine. Say something sure to make potential customers hesitate to call him back. For example, "Hi, this is (mark's name). I can't come to the phone now because I'm having sex with my (secretary, hand, child, retarded cousin, kitten, neighbor's German shepherd . . .).

APARTMENTS

- Squirt some Eastman 910 (or similar) glue into the lock on your mark's apartment door when she's out for the evening. She will not only not be able to get back into her apartment, she will also create a disturbance trying to do it.
- If your mark lives in an older apartment that has wooden door frames, at night you can quietly and quickly lock him in the apartment from the outside by attaching a hasp and keeper on the door and frame with wood screws. Then finish the job by slipping a padlock through the loop and quietly walking away.
- Take out a classified ad to sublet your mark's apartment. Request that calls be made in the wee hours to accommodate an unusual work shift. List either the mark's phone number or his landlord's.
- Periodically set a large array of empty booze bottles outside your target's apartment door.
- Send a bogus letter to your mark's neighbors from either a pest control company or a fictitious health department employee. Have the letter say that you are writing to advise them that your mark's apartment has been found to be infested with the rapacious Venezuelan cockroach. Go into detail about the damage they can

cause or the diseases they can carry and say that it is vital that authorities be notified if the infestation spreads. Describe the insect in some detail, making sure the description could look kinda like your everyday, common variety cockroach.

APPOINTMENTS

- Make appointments for the victim with doctors, dentists, lawyers, and psychiatrists. Many of these professionals charge for visits even it no one shows up. If you know the names of the victim's personal doctor, dentist, etc., set up the appointments with them, which will make it difficult for him to see them when he really needs to.
- If your victim is a saleswoman, have people call and make bogus appointments to meet her at various places—restaurants, clubs, and so on. To keep her waiting longer, have your accomplices leave a message saying they were delayed and will be half an hour late.

APRIL FIRST

- Take the day off. Everyone deserves a day of rest.

ARSON

- If you've been fired to create a spot for someone who would count toward a company's affirmative action quota and feel like doing some firing of your own, here's something for you. To create the illusion of an unsuccessful but serious attempt at arson, wedge a cigarette in a matchbook with the burned-out end sticking out. Collect an appropriate amount of cigarette

ashes to drop under the cigarette at the "arson" scene. Leave this device at the scene, sitting on top of a pile of gasoline-soaked rags that can't be traced back to you. Leave and call the fire department from a pay phone. Disguise your voice because the call will be recorded.

ASSASSINATION

- Threaten the life of a politician by telegram and in your mark's name. The FBI, CIA, and Secret Service keep lists of those who have threatened political figures and often jail them, keep them under protective custody, or place them on 24-hour surveillance when political targets are in the area. This will also work with state officials, bringing a visit from state police or other law enforcement officials.

ATHLETICS

- If your mark is into playing games, slap a dose of analgesic balm or Sea Breeze into his jockstrap pocket.

AUTO DEALERS

- If a dealership screws you over, get even by waiting outside the showroom until a prospective customer starts talking to a salesperson about the same type of car you got. Walk up to the customer and tell him your story in a cool, honest, good-citizen manner. Screw up as many potential sales as you can in this way. Anticipate the manager asking you to leave and alert the local newspaper or television station action line reporters. When the manager asks you to leave and you don't, he will probably call the police. While he does that, you call your reporter. You will get your message across to a lot of people who are either reading or viewing the news.

- A bottle opener can cause damage to a vehicle's finish.
- Various additives can be put into a vehicle's fuel tank.
- If you can find a way to transport roadkill without getting yourself dirty, stuff some under the front seat or in the glove compartments of display room cars.
- Leave a used condom in the backseat of a new car or in a customer's car in the service garage.
- If you can find a way to sneak into the dealer's service area with a backpack full of sabotage paraphernalia (glue, wire cutters, paint, potatoes, M80s), quickly and quietly destroy the dealer's service reputation.

AUTOMOBILES

- Place a bunch of old nuts and bolts into the wheel well behind the hubcap of your mark's car. The noise will make him think his car is falling apart.
- Loosen or remove some lug bolts from your mark's car wheel. The wheel will roll off the car in short order.
- Place a fisherman's split-shot sinker on the accelerator cable of your mark's vehicle after first extending the cable. The lead weight should go on the extended portion. This effectively blocks the cable from returning and runs the throttle wide open.
- It will take a locksmith to get into a car that has had superglue squirted into its keyholes. A more costly (to the mark) version of this trick is to break off an old key in the car door locks before adding the superglue.

- Prop some large-headed nails against the tires of your mark's vehicle when it's parked in such a way that it will have to be backed up to leave the parking stall.
- If you can get to the distributor cap, remove it and use graphite from a pencil to contact the rotor brushes. The charge will run along the graphite causing the engine to misfire. Your mark will probably take the car for an unnecessary tune-up.
- Drop a couple of Alka Seltzer tablets or some bicarbonate of soda into the terminals of your mark's car battery. They will neutralize the battery acid as well as its power.
- Use a pushpin and jab a few holes through your mark's spark plug wires. This will cause a loud rumbling noise when the car is driven.
- Adding silicone carbide, emery powder, fine metal filings, ground cork, resins, and other similar additives to an automobile engine can cause a mechanical breakdown.
- Add a gallon of shellac thinner to your target's gasoline tank. The alcohol will gather all the water in the fuel trap, and when this mixture goes through the fuel line, it will make the vehicle snort and stammer and sound like it has carburetor problems. But the problem will be gone by the time your mark drives the car to the mechanic. Do this several times and your mark will look like quite an idiot.
- Add styrene to the crankcase of your target's vehicle to completely break down the oil and ruin the engine. This is better than sugar in the gas tank because it can't be seen after being introduced and because a little goes a long way. One pint per four quarts of oil will allow the vehicle to run about 100 miles before the engine locks up.
- If your mark parks his car with the rear end toward his house, wait until it's cold outside and stuff a hard potato tightly into the car's

exhaust pipe. When the mark starts the car and waits for the engine to warm up, the hot gases will build up and eventually shoot that hot potato right into the side of the mark's house, perhaps making holes or, at the very least, denting the siding.

- Shove a firecracker, an M80, or a shotgun shell into your mark's exhaust pipe using a stiff wire until the device falls into the muffler. A few minutes of driving will create hot exhaust gases that will cause the explosive device to blow up.

- Strategically wedge a pair of sexy lady's panties between the cushions of your mark's backseat. (The ultimate wedgy!) Before leaving them there, you might spray them with a little perfume. Or leave some light-colored men's bikini briefs decorated around the fly with a few smeared lipstick prints. Have a trusted female friend call a few times and ask nervously to speak to the mark.

- If your mark is a woman, hide (but not very well) an opened package of condoms in her car. Or leave some handkerchiefs that have been heavily impregnated with semen scrunched up in the corner of the backseat. Then, place a series of telephone calls from a nervous male at a time you suspect your mark's husband would be answering the phone.

- If your mark is in the habit of going to the movies alone, follow him one night and when the movie begins, hot-wire the car and drive to an area with nice homes and manicured yards, preferably close to the theater. Drive the car over the yards, digging out the grass and driving over shrubs and flower beds. Drive over the lawn furniture and mailboxes and generally make a mess of the yard. Do this quickly (make sure someone sees the car) and get the car back to the theater parking lot. Park the car and leave. Police have a real problem with the "but, officer, I was at the movies alone" alibi.

- Remove the license plate from your mark's car. She will be stopped by the police.

- Carry a pellet pistol (a compressed air gun) and a supply of .177 caliber pellets in your car. Next time some jerk pulls his vehicle out in front of you or cuts you off, pull up behind him and get in his blind spot. Plunk a few shots into his vehicle—the trunk of a car, or the back of a van or semi. This will make a loud *thwunk* when the pellet hits a van or car, so be careful. Big trucks are so loud, the driver will probably never hear the noise. After your attack, go on about your business. If nothing else, this will alleviate some of your frustration.

- While your mark is dining out or seeing a movie with his wife, leave a note on the passenger side of his windshield saying: "Hi, Doll! Recognized your car but couldn't wait for you. Friday night's still on, right? Luv ya.—Sherri."

- Add linseed oil to your mark's crankcase. Linseed oil oxidizes and dries out, so instead of lubricating the moving parts, it binds them up.

- Drain the oil from your mark's crankcase and fill it with water. The water will stop the oil warning light from coming on, leaving your target in ignorance until the engine seizes.

- Remove a couple of spark-plugs from your mark's car, drop a few small ball bearings into the cylinders, and then replace the plugs. This will really ball things up.

- Drop a small amount of solvent into the master cylinder of your target's brake system. This will slowly eat away all rubber parts, causing a gradual, expensive, totally unstoppable breakdown of the brakes.

- If your mark has a designated parking spot, go to a junkyard and buy a newly crushed wreck and arrange to have it transported to your target's normal parking spot. Co-ordinate the time the wreck is delivered to your moving your mark's car a couple of parking places away.

- Get your hands on an uncrushed wreck that is similar to your mark's car and coordinate moving your mark's car with the delivery of the wreck to your mark's assigned parking space. Pour a little gasoline over the wreck, toss a match, and disappear fast.
- Fill the glove compartment, engine compartment, trunk, or entire interior of your mark's car with expanding insulation foam.
- Add battery acid, salt, sugar, yeast, flour, quick-cooking rice, or black pepper to your mark's car radiator. Any of them will clog up the cooling passages.
- Pour pancake batter over your target's engine block just after the car's been used and the engine is still hot.
- Place raw chicken parts or fish heads in the trunk of your target's car or in the cracks of the seats, or pour a pint of milk over the carpets on a hot summer day. Leave the rest to nature.
- Create a cardboard stencil with an appropriate message and set it on your mark's plastic dashboard. Fill the holes with nail-polish remover, which has a nice tendency to eat into all kinds of plastic.
- Spread some quick-drying glue and a sprinkle of abrasive along the length of your mark's windshield wipers. It's sure to give him a different view of things.
- Wrap your target's car with plaster-impregnated bandages used for making emergency casts for broken limbs. Next dump a few buckets of water over your handiwork, and in 10 minutes or so the wet bandages will set like rock.
- Dump a quantity of used engine oil under your target's car, taking care to smear some on the oil pan. Your target will think he's got a leak and will waste time and money at the garage.
- To ensure that your target consistently overfills his oil, saw half an inch off the dipstick. Overfilling the oil causes real leaks and splits in the seals.
- If you happen to see a parking ticket on your mark's windshield, remove the ticket, doctor it in some offensive way, and send it to the authorities without the fine.
- If your mark has a relatively small car, enlist a few friends to help you lift and carry the car to a spot where it's going to be almost impossible to drive out, or to a place where it will be difficult to get into (between two closely planted trees, for example). Or move it to a restricted parking area and call the police. If you can get a couple more friends to help, you could turn the car upside down.
- Puncture your mark's tires and glue up the lug nuts.
- When your target is parked nose-to-nose with another car, use some strong fishing line and tie the cars together by looping the line several times through the front grills. Whoever moves first will rip out either his own or the other car's grill—possibly both.
- Sprinkle the roof of your target's car with birdseed and let nature take its course.
- Squirt your mark's car with brake fluid—a couple of coats should be enough to make the finish disappear.
- Coat your target's car with epoxy and stick newspapers all over it.
- Using a jeweler's drill and a glass-cutting bit, drill tiny holes in beam headlights of your target's car. Now, using a hypodermic syringe, inject gasoline, lighter fluid, spray butane, or the like into the holes. Reseal the holes with wax, clay, gum, or something that will prevent fumes from escaping.

When the target turns on the headlights, it will activate incendiary devices that will either explode, shoot flames from the front of the car, or completely take the front fenders off, depending on the amount of chemical injected.

- On a day when rain is forecast, check the victim's car to see if he's locked it. If not, roll down the windows and open the sun roof if he has one.

- Fill your mark's gas tank with popcorn. The gauge will read "full," will be full, but the fuel won't be available. After he stalls, fuel will eventually seep out (depending on what sort of gas pickup device his tank has), and he'll be able to go again—for a while.

- Tightly roll a dinner-plate-size piece of black plastic sheet and stuff it in your target's gas tank. It will float around in the tank, eventually getting sucked up against the pickup screen and shut him down. After he stalls out, it will fall off, and he'll be able to proceed for a while.

- A 15-cent wire tie (self-locking plastic strap electricians use to harness wires together and cops use to "flex-cuff" prisoners) will create a rhythmic noise that will convince your mark something is about to fall off her new car. Strap it tightly to the drive shaft so the tip of it will slap the undercarriage. If it's a front-wheel-drive with no drive shaft, you can loop the wire through the wheel, where it will slap the frame or fender.

- Get a glass-etching kit from a hobby shop and write your victim an irremovable message on his windshield. Be sure to write it in reverse so your mark will have no trouble reading it.

- Paint a thin line of copper paint down the insulator of your target's spark plugs to connect metal with metal.

- Dressed appropriately, follow your target to one of those snazzy, snobby restaurants that features valet parking. You know, the kind that's too proper to issue receipts. After your target goes into the restaurant, stroll over to one of the valets who didn't park your target's car, flashing a five or ten-dollar tip in your hand and summon "your" vehicle. Describe your target's vehicle briskly and even recite the license number if asked. The kid will deliver your target's car, and you're on your way. Park it a couple blocks away in a no-parking zone.

- If you have a neighbor who likes to get drunk and do some four-wheelin' in your yard at night, chances are, he's similarly offended some other neighbors. Enlist some help from fellow offendees and wait until the next time your mark parks his four-wheel-drive and crawls inside to pass out in a drunken stupor. Then build a fort around the offending vehicle using logs and mortar. By the time your mark wakes up, the mortar will be dry.

- If you want to ensure that your mark keeps his car in the garage for a while, generously apply some Liquid Nail all the way around the gaps and seams between the garage door, frame, and jamb. It will set and seal overnight.

BALLOONS

- If you've tried everything you can think of to get a particular asshole off your back, but he continues to get drunk and harass you in front of your friends, arm yourself with a Bullybusting Ammonia Balloon Fist. Just force enough ammonia into an ordinary kid's balloon to bulge the rubber pretty well (about two cups). Next time the jerk starts shoving you around, smack him in the face with the ammonia balloon. Provided he still can, he'll think twice next time about giving you the business.

BANKCARDS

- ATM ever eat your card for no reason at all? Find a way to get hold of a blank plastic bankcard, and paint copper on its surface in the form of a grid. Be careful that the line groups don't touch each other. Do both sides of the card and make sure that the contact points from each side meet at the same points and at the edge of the card. Now carefully connect the wires of a Taser Stun Gun to the points at the edge of the card. Take your device to the hungry ATM and zap the stun gun. Memorable last supper.

BANKS

- Get hold of some cheap foreign coins that are the same size as a quarter. Get some paper coin wrappers and wrap the foreign coins in the middle and some real quarters on the ends. Wear a business suit and take the rolled coins to the target bank during its busiest time. They will most likely give you $10 per roll without checking the contents.
- Posing as the target bank's ad manager, call a college newspaper and place some advertisements that offer student benefits such as no service sharge, no minimum balance, and free checks. Say the bank is giving away free concert tickets or CDs for opening an account.
- If your target bank has money machines, (and now days, what banks don't?) buy some hard cheese and cut it to the size and shape of your bank card. Insert the cheese into the credit card slot and leave the bank wondering who cut the cheese.
- If you really want to make a stink at a bank that's been giving you trouble, rent a safe deposit box under a fake name. Buy some near-ripe fresh fish at the grocery store, wrap them in plastic, and carry them in your briefcase to the bank. Ask to access your safe deposit box and say that you will need a few minutes and would like a privacy

cubicle. Once you're there, unwrap the fish and make your deposit.

- Superglue pens to the desks in the bank foyer or feed superglue-covered bank cards into the money machines.
- To put a scare into a particularly rude cashier, burst into the bank lobby on a busy afternoon wearing a ski mask and gloves and rush up to the counter in an extremely aggressive fashion. Thrust a note to the cashier while glaring menacingly at customers and other employees. The note should read: "Please, can you change this $50 bill for me? I have a taxi waiting."
- Gum up automatic teller machines by using doggy doo or feeding in a card coated with superglue. Do this to all the bank's branch machines in a wide area just before a holiday weekend.
- Spread roofing nails around in the parking area used by bank customers.
- To allow yourself about three extra days to get money in the bank to cover a check you've just written, prick pinholes between the numbers at the bottom of the check—the area where the machine scans/reads it. The pinholes shut all of that down, causing a real human to have to process the check. And we all know how long it takes a real person to do anything anymore.
- Fed up with nasty tellers at the drive-up window? Instead of checks, deposits, payments, and other bank documents, load the vacuum tube with wasps, fleas, mold spores, fire ants, and so on. Drive away before she can ask for identification.

BAR BANDS

- If you're a member of a bar band and are fed up with the bullshit you have to put up with

from local drunks, improvise some lyrics and make up impromptu songs about their ugly pusses, breath, IQ, choice of companions, whatever. Their remaining brain cells may not function well enough to make them realize they're the star of the song, but, hell, it'll make you feel a little better.

- If your band has been cheated on your cut of the house, make calls to various booking agents on behalf of your mark's bar or music club and cancel upcoming shows. Or make bookings for bands that somehow don't make the date.

BARS

- If you see your victim in a watering hole that employs a bouncer, pay a couple of female barflies to complain to the bouncer that the guy is harassing them. Bouncers love their job.
- If you're a woman and are trying to have a drink with a woman friend in a bar, and some schmuck scumbag keeps hitting on you, oblivious to your repeated attempts to turn him off, give in. Ask him if he would like to play a new game with you and your friend called "ChiChi." Tell him that the only rule of the game is that he has to do everything to your friend that you do to him. The horny sleaze will jump at the chance. Inconspicuously palm the contents of an ashtray and then stroke your fingers horizontally across his forehead, saying, "ChiChi." He'll do it to your friend. Now you do the same thing, only to his chin, then to his cheeks, and so on. Finally, finish your drinks and leave without a word. Mr. Macho will just stand there looking like an ash.

BATHROOMS

- Get a friend to go to the victim's home posing as a salesman. While he's there have him ask to use the facilities, and when he's in the bathroom have him stuff a washcloth far down into the commode. This will cause the commode to overflow bountifully and without warning.
- Purchase some small pieces of graphite or a spoonful or so of graphite dust from a hardware store and gain access to your target's shower. Remove the shower head and dry the inside, slip the graphite in, and screw the head back in place. Next time your target uses the shower, he will be covered from head to toe in black graphite solution. As an added bonus, the shower will also be a nice mess.
- Remove the shower head in your mark's shower, slip in a couple of bouillon cubes or a block of solid poster paint, and then screw the shower head back on.
- Smuggle a syringe full of garlic oil into your target's bathroom and inject it into the toothpaste or squirt in into the bottle of mouthwash.

BATHTUBS

- If you really want to roast your mark, put two jars of commercial meat tenderizer in her bathwater before a romantic evening out. The evening will have to be called off because the tenderizer is a hell of an irritant.

BB MACHINE GUN

- There is a BB machine gun sold through the mail by a specialty outfit in Florida that is a formidable glass-trashing device. If your target makes a practice of borrowing the boss' car for his own personal use when the boss is out of town, a couple-second drive-by with the BB machine gun while the target's dropping off his laundry will make him the target of the boss' angry curiosity.

BETTER BUSINESS BUREAU

- If the victim is a business owner, repeatedly report him to the Better Business Bureau as a cheat and a crook. Get different people to complain, if you can. This should ruin his business reputation.

BICYCLES

- Use metal cutters to remover the padlock from your mark's bicycle and replace it with a look-alike.

BIKERS

- Toss a length of chain into the spokes of a dirt bike when it's passing by. The bike will stop instantly, but the rider continues his journey forward.
- Use wire cutters to cut bike spokes.
- Pour a patch of grease on the dirt bike path.
- Let the air out of the tires.
- Put additives (see above) in the gas tanks of dirt bikes.

BILLBOARDS

- No doubt about it, a billboard can really throw an ugly kink into an otherwise serene country setting. Can't beat 'em? Then join 'em by painting over their advertising headlines and inserting your own balloon/caption combinations. For example, on a billboard that shows a man and a woman smoking a well-known brand of cigarettes and staring longingly into each other's eyes, have the man saying to the woman, "My doctor says I've got two months to live, how 'bout you?"

BOATS

- Know someone who always puts the damper on your water-skiing enjoyment by driving his oversized, overloud speedboat too close to yours? Make a few waves of your own. Next time he docks the boat at a marina bar to hoist a few, chain Mr. Mark's boat with a heavy chain under the water, to the bar's dock and social platform. After a couple of drinks, count on your mark to jump in his boat and take off full-throttle . . . trailing his bar behind him.

BOMBS

- To create a stink bomb that has been said to "melt the doors off Ft. Knox," mix powdered hydrogen sulfide with vinegar and let it dry to a paste. Next, very carefully remove some gunpowder from an M80 or homemade firecracker and replace some of the powder with the dried paste in a 50/50 ratio. When the firecracker is detonated, the loud explosion will be followed by a major cloud that will smell far worse than any death fart.

BOOBY TRAPS

- Remove the contents from some of those silly gag peanut-brittle cans that spring snakes jump out of and reload them with raw eggs, used condoms, beef blood, football player snot, and some other truly gross stuff. Leave them as party favors at your mark's next party.
- You can make nitrogen tri-iodide (NI_3) by mixing equal volumes of common household iodine and ammonia and stirring thoroughly. It's totally safe as long as you KEEP IT WET. Dry, this stuff is temperamental under its own weight. Apply some of the liquid NI_3 to your mark's toilet seats, car doors, car tires—any area where there could be contact detonation.
- When your mark has really hurt you and you think she deserves to cry, buy one of those highly effective hand-held tear-gas sprayers and spray her apartment doorknob, car door handles, telephones, toilet seat, whatever. It stays active for several hours, and when it comes in contact with skin it provides a burning sensation for a half an hour or so.
- If your mark is a hard-core snoop who just has to open books, boxes, drawers, or letters, load an empty videotape box with a small smoke bomb triggered by a simple pressure-relief switch. Mark the tape box PERSONAL—DO NOT OPEN! and leave it where your target can't miss it. Curiosity won't kill this cat, but it'll give 'em a scare.

14

BOOKS

- Ever loan someone a book that he didn't return? Here's a way to make that book-worm really squirm. Have a printer make a couple dozen bookplates with your mark's name and address and the announcement: "If this book is lost and you return it, I will pay you $10 cash." Next, purchase some hardback books at a garage sale and paste the bookplates on the inside front cover. Then lose the books—at the park, in a bus, or in a restaurant or bar.
- Introduce silverfish to your mark's library. They love nothing better than a good book, except maybe a bunch of good books.
- Donate books in your mark's name to the local library. Not just any books, of course. Get some really sleazy illustrated porno books and go back to your friendly printer to order yet another set of bookplates. This time they should say something like, "This book donated to the [fill in the name] library by [fill in mark's name] in loving memory of the little kids (or the sheep or Shetland ponies) of [fill in town name]."

BOOZE

- Find a way to slip some Anabuse to your mark before he goes out for cocktails. It won't kill him, it'll just make him wish he were dead.
- If you have some freeloading neighbors who always invite themselves to your keg parties and to your keg, and never offer to reciprocate, next time they're a laundry load to the wind, mix a little urine in with their next pitcher of beer. They'll never know—it looks the same, and by that time they won't be tasting anyway.

- Refill apple cider jugs with stale beer and stick them in your mark's refrigerator.

BOUNTY HUNTERS

- Look through the dozens of relatively recent "Wanted" posters in the post office for some nasty criminal who looks like your mark. Borrow it and make Xerox copies to which you affix a notary seal. Now show your mark's poster around macho bars where amateur bounty hunters and other *Soldier of Fortune* subscribers hang out, indicating that there's a $25,000 reward for this person. Mention that he was last seen in the vicinity of your mark's neighborhood.

BUGS— ELECTRONIC

- Covertly plant a small wireless receiver/speaker somewhere inopportune for your mark and then, using a transmitting radio, do some transmitting over that speaker. You could do it in a fast-food restaurant that has offended you. Call out additional or confusing orders or contribute social, ethnic, or racial comments that will offend some of the customers.
- If you don't have a particular mark in mind and just want to have a little fun at some unsuspecting stranger's expense, plant a bug in the stall of a woman's rest room and monitor the patrons entering the facility from your car. Wait for a large lady to go in and give her enough time to get fully into operation, and then shout into the transmitter: "Ohhh, ouch, geez, lady, move your lard ass. You're smashing me. I can't breathe. Damn

you, you tonnablubber, get your fat ass off my head." Do this at your own risk. Mad fat ladies can be downright vengeful.

BUGS—LIVING (OR RECENTLY LIVING)

- Buy a box of bees from a beekeeper and carefully introduce them into your target's home through the letter box or a hole in a screen.
- Collect some cockroaches, earwigs, and wood lice and mail them first class (so they don't have time to die) to your target. Leave a business card on the door offering the services of an exterminator.
- So your neighbor raises horses and can't quite seem to keep the horseflies to home? Gain access to his house and strategically place small pieces of liquid fly bait on top of the door and window frames, behind curtains, in flower pots, on shelves, ceiling lights and chandeliers, and so on. Once the house has been thoroughly baited, use a pencil point to enlarge interstices in all of the target's screens to ensure that the flies can come home to papa.
- If you want to attract clouds of annoying fruit flies to your mark's yard in the summer, water down some applesauce and pour it in the grass where people won't notice it.

BULLIES

- Call the victim's toughest neighbor, tell him you work down at the local bar (restaurant, garage) and that the victim has been down there badmouthing him. If you know of a

specific squabble between the two of them, say the victim was talking about that when he made his disparaging remarks.
- If a bully has been mistreating your teenager by stealing his lunch money, cigarettes, notebook paper, and so on, load a few cigarettes with gunpowder, and next time the bully steals the cigarettes, he'll get firsthand experience that smoking is truly bad for his health.
- Print some handbills saying "You've Messed with the Rest, Now Lose to the Best," and put your target's name and address at the bottom of the flyer. Post them at every karate school and tough-guy bar you can find.
- Sneak a small camera into the locker room where some bully jocks are cleaning up after a game. Take a couple of candid shots of the naked boys doing a little grab-ass. Plaster prints of the shenanigans all over the school, but first add sexual request captions to the photos.
- If your mark is a macho woman-beater, get him good and drunk, then feed him a little sleeping potion to secure the condition. Dress him in drag and shoot a lot of semi-nude photos showing his made-up face, him blowing one of the guys, and fully nude shots in compromising positions with an amorous mastiff. Re-dress him and take him home. A few days later send the photos to his office, parent's home, favorite bar, girlfriend's home . . .

BUMPER STICKERS

- If your mark has a bumper sticker that says "Shit Happens," make up one of your own and plaster it to the right of his. Yours might read, "I'm Living Proof."
- Put bumper stickers on your mark's car that say things like "Kill Cops," "Bikers Blow It

Out Their Ass," anything that will draw some not-so-friendly attention.

- Put a sticker on your own vehicle that says, "I Brake for Tailgaters," and hook a toggle switch up to your brake lights. Flip the switch when someone starts to ride your bumper. Maybe they'll start believing what they read.

BUREAUCRATS

- On the Fourth of July, raise the flag of a communist country on your bureaucrat target's roof.
- Register your patriotic bureaucratic mark with a variety of extremist political groups. He will be harassed from both extremes—the organization he unwittingly "joined" and the police.
- If your target works for the police or government security, or is in the armed forces, acquire some letterhead from the offices of a potentially hostile power (send a query to the consulate asking about visa requirements to get a letter back and make

your own blanks) and send bizarre cryptic coded letters to your target at work. For example, say "Sunday, 1 P.M., Rushdie" from the "Iranians."

BUSINESS REPLY MAIL

- When you receive solicitations through the mail asking for money or supplies for organizations that particularly get your goat, fill a few old gasoline tanks with used motor oil, package them well, and mark the parcel EMERGENCY MEDICAL SUPPLIES—PRIORITY MAIL. Now slap their postage-paid, business reply envelope on the parcel and mail it to them.

BUTANE LIGHTERS

- Butane lighters will explode if exposed to sparks, fire, or intense heat. Don't shove butane lighters into your mark's automobile muffler.

CABLE TELEVISION

- If you're in an area where you can use your Touch Tone telephone to obtain pay-per-view cable service, use a pay phone and call the cable company. Follow the instructions given by the automated voice and then dial in your mark's phone number. You can purchase any number of events for your mark that he will discover later have been billed to him.

- If you're tired of poor service from your cable company and can't switch to another one because it's the only game in town, do what you can to ensure others won't sign up and get burned. Make a few late night calls heckling and hassling would-be customers to subscribe to the service or send phony bills on fake invoices to noncustomers, including some government big shots.

CAMPING

- Get into a conversation with the rude, unruly campers who have pitched their tent all too close to yours. Bring up the "snake problem" at that campsite. Tell the mark that the snakes aren't really a problem because they come out only at night when everyone is inside his camper or tent, all zipped up and snakeproof. Then say, "Besides, I don't believe that rumor about people being bitten by snakes this past week."

- If you camp next to a group that has a loud, nonstop party all night, the following morning, while they sleep it off, swipe all their firewood and put a few sticks in a nearby poison ivy patch. When they begin their party the next night and look for firewood, they'll figure they used it all the previous night and go scouting for more. At dusk you can still see firewood. Poison ivy's not so recognizable.

- If your mark is camping in bear country, be sure to rub ground beef or sardine oil all over the roof of his car at night. Mix in some honey, too.

CAMPUS

- If they charge too much in your dormitory laundry rooms, dump a couple of double cheese and pepperoni pizzas into the dryers and turn them on.

- If you have a professor you don't like, and he lectures from a desk or podium on a raised platform, move the stand so its legs are barely balanced on the front edge of the platform. When teach leans forward, the structure will come crashing down, most likely with teacher in tow.

- Stuff a few geese in a stuffy professor's office closet at night. By morning when she opens the closet door, those ruffled geese will fluff her pillow.

- If you're a faculty member and you have an especially difficult-to-deal-with colleague, send nasty, personal, and vindictive memoranda to other staff members or the deans in the name of your difficult colleague. Or send nasty letters bearing school letterhead to the parents of a few of that faculty member's students. Discuss the students' questionable genetic makeup and resultant academic abilities. Use your colleague's signature stamp at the letters' closings.

- If you know of one of those rich-kid, do-nothing students who buys his term papers already written, while the rest of the students sweat over their own term papers, plagiarize a few semiobscure essays and poems from some dust-covered literature books in the college library. Type them up under the rich kid's name and submit them to the campus literary magazine for publication. The thing about semiobscure is that you can bet there'll be some stuffy old literature professor on campus who'll recognize the stuff and make it his business to look into the matter.

CANDY

- Here's a way to get those candy thieves at the office who won't take a chocolate when you're watching; but will empty your candy box the minute your back is turned. Collect dead insects from dusty window sills, cover the little corpses with chocolate, and put them in the box with the real candy. Remember what Forrest Gump's mama said: "Life is like a box of chocolates—you never know what you're gonna get."

- Collect a little dog doo that has dried in the sun for a couple of days. (This will not be a difficult task.) Wearing rubber gloves, cut

the crap (so to speak) into pieces the size of cherries. Next, melt some milk chocolate in a double boiler and gently dip the shit (so to speak) in the melted milk chocolate. When they're dry, wrap each one in a piece of that golden foil that real chocolate-covered cherries come in. Fill a candy box with them and reseal the box. Have an accomplice smuggle the little treats into your target's cocktail party.

CARBIDE

- When calcium carbide is exposed to air and water, it produces a gas that will kill small animals.

- Water and carbide can produce an explosion. Put a pound or two of carbide into a can, seal it, and punch a few holes in the lid. It can do interesting things to your mark's goldfish pond or indoor aquarium.

- Put a carbide bomb into a toilet, leave a lighted cigarette on the seat, and run as if your life depended on it. The carbide will combine with water to produce a cloud of noxious gas, which will explode when it comes in contact with the lighted cigarette. This carbide bomb can do more damage than an M80.

- A pound or so of carbide dumped into the toilets of corporate or government buildings and flushed into the system can cause a dangerous backup of gases.

- A combination of water and carbide when fed into the ventilating systems of corporate or government buildings will give the bureaucrats an unexpected day off.

CAR DEALERS

- If you've been sold a lemon and have

access to a computer graphics package, scan in an advertisement for the car dealership. Next drop an image of a lemon in an appropriate spot on the picture of the dealer's lot. Have the new image printed up as postcards and do a mail drop in the dealer's area.

- If you feel you've gotten shoddy service from the car-leasing department of a car dealership, send your last monthly payment in pennies in a large box, with a note saying, "This is what I think your service is worth." Don't put postage on the box and use the dealer's address as the return address. It will have to pay the postage.

CAREERS

- If you're a professor and know of some students who have continually abused their privileges, paid or bullied others into doing their work for them, cheated and scammed the school and fellow students, and otherwise made obnoxious fools of themselves, write reference letters for the little jerks, informing prospective employers the truth and nothing but the truth about their sorry asses. Then sign some bogus professor's name and send the letters to the job placement office. Some overworked clerk will stamp them in and file them without a second thought to the bogus signature.

CASSETTE TAPES

- Tape over your mark's music cassettes with anything you know he would find offensive.

CB RADIOS

- To teach your neighborhood CBer who refuses to filter his equipment and thus disrupts TV, stereo, AM/FM, and other normal communication transmissions a lesson, wait until the mark is away from the area. Unfasten the CB coax line from the antenna, then clip two leads of regular 110 volt line to the CB coax—one lead to the center conductor, the other to the shield. Small alligator clips will work for this. Plug the other end of the 110 volt into your mark's nearest outdoor socket. The next time he turns on the CB and hits the transmit button, even the repair people will be at a loss about what to do.

- Poke a tiny pin through the plastic outer cable of the coax and through the shield, making sure it touches the core. Cut the head off the pin and push it in until it is out of sight and close the plastic behind the pin to hide the hole. Repeat this procedure a couple more times along the coax between the antenna and CB set. All future transmissions will be unclear and stuttery.

- To pay back that overpainted office hussy at the office who seduces married men and calls their wives to report the affairs, pretending to be you or some other female co-worker, dig out your old CB, hook it up, and go out on some high open ground near a popular truck stop. In your sexiest voice, pitch yourself as the Highway Hooker. Using short transmissions at random times, advertise yourself as the finest, warmest, best lay-lady in five states. Give out the office hussy's phone number.

- Pack a mobile FM or AM transmitter with a maximum range of about 100 feet in your car. Then when some driver's ed dropout frightens or threatens you with unacceptable driving, you use your mobile transmitter to overpower whatever station he has on the radio and monologue his poor driving.

- If your mark has graduated from CB to ham radio, and you can get his license call letters and access to a radio to use, you can have a lot of fun. Play funky and kinky music, jam out repeaters and simplex operations, keep giving his call sign over the air, talk dirty, and then tauntingly dare other ham operators to track you down. Abuse them and their mothers verbally. Just be ready to make tracks. CBers are some of the best trackers there are.

CEMETERY

- Badger the telephone company and the local cemetery in the name of your target, making all sorts of wild requests for a special telephone hookup for his casket. Explain that you have this fear of being buried alive. Keep it up for months.

CHAIN SAWS

- If you know your mark is about to buy a chain saw, find an accomplice in the store to offer counseling, humor, advice, old leftovers . . .

CHARITY

- Volunteer your mark's services to various charities' recruiters, providing them her name, address and phone number. Other volunteers will show up at the mark's door with campaign and collection materials.
- Call during telethons and other charity

drives and make generous pledges in your mark's name.

- Call in pledges to especially irritating telethons that announce contributors' names over the air using double-entendre names like Seymour Butts, Connie Lingus, Peter Small, Ura Nass.
- Call your local Salvation Army or Goodwill and report your mark for stealing out of the organization's pickup boxes. Give your mark's license plate number.
- Does your mark hassle anyone on relief, welfare, food stamps? Set her up as a buyer of food stamps (illegal in most states) by posting flyers offering 70 cents on the dollar. If you can, lard her apartment with about $40 worth of food stamps to make it more convincing to the authorities who will arrive soon after you anonymously notify them.

CHEESE

- Spread Limburger cheese on the muffler or exhaust manifold of a new car. Or put some behind a radiator in a home or office. After it's turned on, the sour smell can last for weeks.

CHEMICALS

- Floc (aka "instant banana peel") is a white powder commonly used to clarify solutions. It is not so commonly used as a riot-control agent because when a little of it is spread on a wet street, nobody can stand up. Does your mark like to dance? Or should we say "slip the light fantastic"?
- Water glass (sodium silicate) is used for coating fresh eggs to preserve them, for fireproofing wood and fabrics, and so on. It can be used for more devious ends, however. For example, drill a hole in the

bottom of a glass and close the hole with several applications of water glass. When your mark makes himself a drink, the water glass plug will dissolve and the drink will be *on* him not *in* him.

- Silver nitrate will turn a redneck black. Find a way to dump some on your bigot target's bath sponge. It might not change his attitude, but it'll give his jive ass a scare.
- Copper sulfate is deadly poisonous to aquatic life and trees. Two pounds dumped into a pond will do the job, while four ounces poured around the drip line—the outer edge of the leaves of any given tree—will murder the tree.
- A 97-percent solution of formaldehyde works as a tear gas substitute for nasty dogs, cats, bats, rats, and so on. Put it in a nasal spray bottle and fire away at any of your animal marks.
- Wrap some lye in a newspaper, fasten it with rubber bands, and then drop or throw it onto your mark's car roof, roof gutters, or any area you want to be eaten through. The lye ruins paint, eats holes in soft metals, stains paint, and kills vegetation.

CHILD ABUSE

- Acting as a concerned neighbor, call the authorities and report your mark as a child abuser. Save this one for someone you want to do enduring damage to—child abuse is such an emotional issue that such an accusation could follow a person for the rest of his life.
- If you spot an accidental cut or bruise on any of the victim's children, report him to the authorities for child abuse. Many cities have child abuse hot lines, and every call prompts an in-depth investigation.

CHILDREN

- Phone the victim just after school hours, say you're the principal of his child's school and you need to discuss an important disciplinary problem with her. Make an appointment to see her at the school at 8 A.M. the next day.

CHRISTMAS TREES

- If your mark's an old scrooge type who gets his rocks off verbally abusing neighbors and their kids and pets, or is always calling the police for things he imagines people are doing to him, a couple of days after Christmas, run and ad in the local paper saying, "If you'd like to recycle your used Christmas trees, please leave them on my driveway or lawn. I will pay up to $3 per tree." Use the old grump's name and address in the ad.

CIA

- Apply for a CIA job in your mark's name, claiming expertise in foreign journalism, foreign languages, and the like, and referencing advanced college degrees and military service abroad.
- Send a letter in the form of a serious cryptogram to some fictional person in Libya, Cambodia, Iraq, North Korea, or some similar "friendly" country. The letter should be addressed to that fictional person at "General Delivery" in some city in that country and should involve a message about assassination, bombs, drugs, or some other topic intended to raise the pulse of a paranoid intelligence officer. Include your

mark's name and home address as the sender of this mysterious missive. If you want to ensure that your letter is intercepted, send it to a fictional character or title at some military or spy institution.

CLASSIFIED ADS

- Call in an ad to sell your irritating neighbor's car. Offer to sell it for less than the market value, indicating a need for quick cash. Ask that calls be placed after midnight because of shift work.
- Put your mark's house up for sale. Ask for calls or visitors at hours that will inconvenience the mark.
- Advertise for "young boy and girl models to pose for 'art' pictures." Leave your mark's home or business telephone number, whichever would cause the most embarrassment.
- Place ads in sleazy tabloids for kinky sex and leave your target's phone number. Buy a copy of the issue that runs the ad and make Xerox copies to send to your mark's neighbors, relatives, business associates, and friends.
- Place an ad for your target in an adult magazine seeking responses from only your mark's particular preference. That might be women over 60, fat women, women with enormous breasts, transsexuals.
- Take out a classified ad in a homosexual publication in which your mark proudly announces his emersion from the proverbial closet. Indicate that he is gay and has dated or married only for cover. Now he wants the world to know he has taken a same-sex lover and name a friend, neighbor, or business associate as that lover. Bear in mind that you could be charged with libel for this should you get caught.
- Use a classified ad to announce an auction of your mark's belongings: "Moving, everything must go. Great bargains!" Run the ad when your mark is out of town and won't read it. Set the time of the auction to begin at 7 in the morning so that your mark is still groggy from sleep. He might even think he's having a nightmare.
- You can place "ads" announcing any number of bizarre ways to harass your mark by posting 3x5 cards on public bulletin boards. These are cheaper than newspaper ads, and they can be more descriptive and personal than ads in publications.
- If your victim advertises something for sale, call and offer him a ridiculously high price for it. Explain that it's something you've always wanted. Ask him to hold it for four days, turning down all other offers, until you can round up the money. After the four days are up, drop him a note letting him know you purposely screwed up his sale.
- Set your target up in business. Place an ad in the paper offering cash for bottle tops, old newspapers, empty tin cans, or any other useless junk you can think of. Make prices attractive and leave the target's home address.
- If a doctor has unnecessarily bled your bank account, take out an ad for her offering to perform cut-rate abortions at home. Or maybe the slimy accountant who messed up your tax return would care to advertise his services under the heading: "Never Pay Taxes Again." Make sure relevant authorities get copies of the ads.
- If your target owns a bookstore, take out a prominent ad for the store in a publication having a high Muslim readership offering signed copies of Salman Rushdie's *Satanic Verses*.
- Use an ad to invite "like-minded" people to

a discussion group at your target's home: a gay-rights discussion group for a bigot, an African Awareness Society for a racist, or a "swingers" experimental group for members of the moral majority.

- If your mark is a woman, place an ad for her offering "Massages by Angel" or "Lingerie Modeling in the Privacy of Your Home."

CLERGY

- Get hold of a nun's habit or priest's robes and wear it to deter suspicion while you carry out any number of actions. They're great for smuggling in the tools of your tricks.
- Call a clergyman to your victim's home to administer last rites.
- Call a minister over to your mark's house to smooth over a domestic squabble. Tell him that you (the victim) and your spouse have been fighting all night, and you're afraid it will end in murder if he doesn't intervene.

CLOTHES

- Add a little methyl violet to your target's laundry detergent to permanently stain her clothing.
- Drop a couple of potassium permanganate crystals down the water reservoir of your mark's steam iron. A press of the steam button will give her a swoosh of deep purple to decorate her crisp white blouse.
- Paint a drop of battery acid on the threads holding buttons on your mark's military uniform. The thread will be weakened to the point where the buttons will drop off on their own with just a little extra strain (like happens when sitting, squatting, or saluting).

- Buy a thread cutter in the fabric section of your local K-Mart and use it to unpick a few stitches at regular intervals in the seams and hems of all your target's clothes. Go for back seams of skirts, seats of pants, armholes of shirts and blouses, and pocket seams.
- If your mark has a favorite item of clothing, wait until she delivers it to the dry cleaner. Call the cleaner posing as your mark's spouse, saying that she was killed in an accident. Say that you found the ticket for the piece of clothing and that you will pay for the cleaning, but that you really couldn't bear to see the piece of clothing again, under the circumstances. Ask the cleaner to donate the item to a local charity so that you don't have to see it when you come to pay the bill.
- If your mark loves to disco, get a security felt-tip pen (whose ink shows up only under ultraviolet light) and write an illuminating message on the seat of your mark's favorite dancin' drawers.
- Squirt your mark's favorite duds with a bit of nitric acid.
- Rub some ski wax on the soles of your mark's shoes in winter and stand back and watch some cross-country ski action.
- If you've been sold a shoddy pair of shoes and the store you bought them from won't make the situation right, return to the store armed with a syringe filled with a mixture of blended cheese spread and alcohol or battery acid. Go at a busy time and ask to try on lots of pairs of shoes. When the opportunity presents itself, surreptitiously inject a good squirt of the juice into the inner soles of as many pairs as possible. Put them back into their boxes and leave. The cheese will get ripe, the acid will rot the thread. Neither circumstance will please future customers.

- Spray some synthetic animal scents used as lures by trappers, hunters, or dog handlers on your target's undergarments. If she's a real bitch, use the scent of a female dog in heat, then stand back and let old rover take over.

CLUBS

- Sign the victim up for book-of-the-month, record-of-the-month, beer-of-the-month, or any other clubs that ship items now and collect later.

COINS

- Use cheap foreign coins that duplicate the size and weight of U.S. coins for use in vending machines, parking meters, telephones, toll gates, Laundromats, and so on. You will finally get reimbursed for all those coins you've lost to unrelenting coin slots in the past.

COLLEGE LIFE

- Get hold of some course withdrawal forms from some office on campus and fill them out in your mark's name.

COMPASSES

- If your mark is a yachtsman, remagnetize the magnets on his yacht backwards.

COMPUTERS

- Pass a portable electromagnet back and forth across computer tapes to erase the information they contain.

- If you can get hold of a stun gun and smuggle it to the location of your target's computer, stun the computer terminal (with around 40,000 volts of punch) and your target will be left with a case of microprocessor meltdown, and probably the vital information he had stored on his hard disk will be scrambled.
- If you can get access to your target's computer manual, the commands to re-format the hard disk should be in there. Have at it.
- Spray your target's 3.5-inch computer disks with some artist's spray adhesive. When the disk is inserted into the disk drive, the adhesive, which remains sticky, will be transferred to the read/write head of your target's computer. Sticky situation indeed.
- When your target is under a stiff deadline, remove one of the key leads from her computer. Or you can mix up the leads among several computers in her office. Either way, no work will get done till things get untangled.
- Remove a few computer chips from your mark's computer and either throw them away, rearrange them, or coat them with clear nail polish to insulate the connection.
- Find a way to introduce one of the many computer viruses into your target's computer.
- Customize your mark's on-screen messages, so that, for example, the "Are you sure you want to delete this file?" query has the addendum "you cheating bastard" tagged on.
- If your target uses his computer for sales meetings, demonstrations, and so on, load in a computer-generated porn program and make sure that whatever key he presses first will cause the program to run.
- Soak your mark's printer paper in 10-percent sulfuric acid. It's invisible, but it will soon crumble a paper supply.

- If you're computer literate, write a self-destruct program into the loop of your mark's computer or set up and program some sort of self-perpetuating mathematical problem that will devour hundreds of hours of undetected—until too late—computer time.

CONTRACTORS

- If a contractor doesn't deliver what was promised and you don't discover it until your house is built, put up a huge sign in your lot that says something like, "Buy this poorly constructed home—CHEAP!" and display the contractor's name and telephone number in a prominent place. When he complains, show him your Xeroxed list of things that are wrong with the house. At the top of the page, state his name, his company's name, address, and telephone number, and a general comment about the poor quality of his work. Have a stack of these lists so he will think you're giving them away to passersby. Your grievances will probably be taken care of quickly.
- If your mark is building anything out of concrete and you have access to the concrete before it is poured, add concentrated hydrochloric acid to it. It causes slow, continual deterioration of a structure because of corrosion.
- On houses under construction, cut the electrical wiring at each receptacle after the insulation is in and just prior to the installation of the wallboard. With the insulation in place, it is next to impossible to see the cut wires, and when the wallboard is in place, the sabotage will not be detected until the owner moves in and tries to use the facilities. Repairs could prove quite costly to your target builder.

CONVENIENCE STORES

- Call your mark convenience store about an hour or so after the newspaper delivery and ask the clerk to hold 10 copies of the newspaper for you (give your secondary mark's name here). Tell the clerk that you'll pick them up within the hour as you're coming from work. At 6:30 call the clerk back and say you were delayed in traffic and are still intending to pick up the newspapers. Apologize and give your secondary mark's name again. Tell the clerk you'll be there by 7:00. At 7:30, call the store back and tell the clerk you don't want the papers anymore because the news is all old. When the clerk raises hell, get abusive and drop the secondary mark's name again and threaten the clerk. It's likely the police will be called.

CONVENTIONS

- Ever had a problem with convention planners? Here's a way to get a little satisfaction. Hire some Rent-A-Clowns to work in addition to the real clowns that always run around at conventions. Dress your clowns the same way, and while the conventional convention clowns are doing gentle, good-natured stuff, your clowns should be spilling people's drinks on other people, honking stuffy society matrons' boobs, pinching asses, spitting on important people, exposing themselves, handing out dirty pictures, and so on. When the commotion really starts, your clowns need to disappear.

CORPORATIONS

- After obtaining the proper letterheads and intelligence information, write a sharply worded business letter from Company A to Company B, demanding payment for merchandise, equipment, and so on. Then, using Company B's "official" letterhead, write Company A a nasty letter complaining of faulty merchandise, equipment, and so on, and threatening personal injury damages from same. Sign the letters with the names and, if possible, the signatures of a middle manager from each company. Mail the letters and await the communication fun.

CREDIT

- Unless your mark is outlandishly wealthy, when he needs to make a major purchase, he has to borrow money, just like the rest of us. You have the power to ensure that your mark won't be able to borrow money. Just obtain a number of those ubiquitous credit applications from stores, shops, restaurants, everywhere. Include legitimate personal information about your mark, except where the form asks for place of employment, write down "Self-Employed" (the phrase "self-employed" stands out unfavorably on a credit application). List income at about $30,000. Where it asks for both home and business telephone numbers, list the home phone for both. Mail a couple of completed cards every 10 days or so. All of this activity will put your mark in the credit-denied category for anywhere from one to four months in most states. If you want, you could start the process all over again in four months.

CREDIT CARDS

- If you can get your victim's credit card number(s), make loads of less than $40 mail order and telephone orders for merchandise. Pretend you are the mark and report the card as having been stolen. She will have a little trouble the next time an attempt is made to use the card.
- Send a letter in your mark's name to his credit card companies saying you want to cancel your cards. Explain that you would have mailed back the cards, but you lost them.

CURSES

- Use a messenger service to send your enemy an object or trinket that supposedly carries a curse or spell. Later have the enemy informed of the curse and let her psyche do the dirty work. You can embellish this by later slashing your mark's tires and leaving another of the same trinkets at the scene. Keep this up as long as you think your enemy is deserving.

DEADBEATS

- If you know someone who's always borrowing money but never paying any back, acquire one of his blank checks, and send a money order to one of those ads that offers 25 personalized checks for five dollars. At the same time, file an address change to a post office box that you open in his name. When you get the checks, make 25 different orders to different mail-order companies and local businesses. Mail the letters. You'll be paid back for all those little loans.

DEATH CERTIFICATES

- If you can obtain a copy of a death certificate, fill it out in your mark's name and mail it to the U.S. Social Security Office in Washington, D.C. This will entangle your mark in a snarl of problems, because it's very hard to convince those folks that you are in fact alive if their information tells them otherwise.
- Send a copy of a death certificate filled out in your mark's name to your county's registrar of voters, and ask the registrar to remove her name from the voting list.

DELICATESSENS

- If you work in a delicatessen and want to get back at those pushy customers who expect and demand everything but to borrow your toothbrush, before you slap that slice of provolone on their sandwich, swat down a couple of flies with it to use as garnish.

DELIVERY OF CONSUMABLES

- From a pay phone, call a place that delivers pizza and give it a fake name in a high rise. When the truck arrives with the order and while the delivery person is in the apartment building trying to locate a nonexistent customer, help yourself to the other pizzas that are in the truck awaiting delivery.
- Call Chinese, Mexican, and Italian restaurants and have them deliver simultaneous orders to the victim's home.

DEPARTMENT STORES

- Send your victim past-due notices from various department store and shops for bills he doesn't really owe. He will have to call and try to get the confusion straightened out, which will cost him lots of time and trouble.

- Follow your victim into a department store. Casually approach a young (more gullible) floor clerk and whisper: "Listen, I don't want to get involved, but that guy over there just stuck some merchandise in his pocket." While he's being detained by security people, buy something small and leave, then drop it in the victim's car outside the store. Security people often search the automobiles of suspected shoplifters.
- Puncture the basketballs in the sporting-goods departments.
- Set up boxes of fishhooks so they spill on the floor.
- If the store sells shot for shotgun shell reloading, cut open a couple of bags in such a way that they won't spill until they are moved.
- Load a blank in the tube magazine of a lever-action rifle. This act could get your sporting-goods manager mark fired.
- To pay a store back for first selling you a cheap piece of furniture that comes unglued or falls apart shortly after delivery and then referring you to the manufacturer somewhere across the country for your complaint, a little motor oil or a small bottle of ink will blend nicely into the middle of a sofa cushion.
- Reverse the wires on stereo speakers, or use a long sharp instrument to puncture the diaphragms.
- Paint pictures on picture tubes to add to the quality of the pictures.

DIAL-A-JOKE

- If your mark is a humorless SOB, take out ads in several local newspapers listing your mark's phone number as the place to call

for a Brand New Off-the-Wall Dial-A-Joke Service, ADULTS ONLY!" You could also list "Dial-A-Prayer" for an atheistic mark, "Dial-A-Nazi" for a Jewish mark or vice-versa; and "Dial-An-Orgasm" for a prudish mark.

DIRTY OLD (AND YOUNG) MEN

- Find yourself a few associates who can act convincingly, making sure one of them is an attractive young woman. Tell the mark that she is married or a daughter, depending on the circumstances, and that she has the hots for your mark. Tell him you will arrange for them to meet, but that he must be cautious since she has a very jealous husband/ protective father. When the night comes for the meeting, have your pretty accomplice scantily dressed as she greets you at the door with a husky, sensual "hello." Give the mark just enough time to size her up and begin to imagine what could come next. Suddenly your second accomplice, preferably a burly fellow, comes running around the side of the house screaming about his wife's/ daughter's honor. You scream convincingly, "Get the hell out of here—it's her husband/ father!" and start to run like a jackrabbit. No doubt you will be followed (or led) by your scuzzy mark. The burly accomplice should fire two shots into the air, and you fall to the ground, screaming "Jeezus, I'm shot! Run like hell!" A little follow-up by a third accomplice, keeping the mark appraised of your condition after the gunshot wound goes a long way.
- Set the dirty old man up with a dirty (diseased) young prostitute.
- Leave a note in feminine handwriting prominently displayed on his front door

saying: "Hi, sweetie. Stopped by again, but it was dark so I didn't knock. Please call right away—we have something important to discuss."

- If your dirty old mark does much international traveling, enlist a lady friend to catch his attention while he is on foreign soil. While she toys with him, find your way to his room and his passport, and stamp every page of it with the word "Deceased." His stay in that foreign country will be compromised, inhospitable, extended, and costly.

- If you have a boss who has the nasty habit of sexually harassing his employees, get hold of his résumé through an accomplice in the personnel division (this probably won't be difficult because these types aren't satisfied with bugging just one lady), make copies of the résumé and send them all over to competitor offices with a personal cover letter "from" your supervisor/mark. In it explain that "I" want a transfer because "my" boss is making homosexual advances toward "me." Then sit back and wait for the information to filter back to your mark's boss.

DISGUISE

- A chemical called bichloride of mercury will give the user a sore throat and will alter the sound of his voice. If your mark is a singer or a politician or businessman scheduled to give an important speech, why not slip a little into that ever-present glass of water?

DOCTORS

- If you're tired of being herded in and out of your doctor's office like a farm animal, after first being made to wait in that cold little room while the doc secures a Wednesday afternoon golf date, make use of the time you spend waiting by removing the inspection stickers from all of the medical equipment in the room. A couple of days later, have a friend with a bureaucratic-sounding voice call the doctor, identify himself as being with the state medical certification board, and mention that there's been a complaint about this doctor using uninspected equipment. Say the patient was talking lawsuit and set up an appointment to discuss the matter, suggesting that the doctor might want to have his attorney present at the meeting. Give them a little taste of what it's like to wait and wonder.

DRUGS

- Obtain a small amount of cocaine and plant it in your mark's car. Then, using a pay phone (and altering your voice by using a recording tape or inhaling some helium just before you make the call), call the police, give them your mark's name and license plate number, and tell them the mark just burned you on a drug deal and you're ticked off and want to report him. Realize that this call will be recorded and could be traced, so make the call quick—no more than 30-45 seconds.

- Call your local "heroin hot line" or similar agency and report the victim as a drug dealer. Tell them he stashes his supply in a secret compartment in his den wall.

- Toss marijuana seeds in the victim's shrubbery. Wait four weeks and tip off the authorities.

- If your victim is vacationing outside the United States, find out where and when he'll re-enter the country and inform the U.S.

Customs office there that he's smuggling narcotics into the country . . . hidden inside a plastic bag stuffed up his rear end.

- If your mark is in the military and works with drug detection canines, rub snuff or red pepper in the vehicle or on his clothing. The substances irritate a dog's nose and will cause the animal to react as if there are drugs present. Sure to raise at least one of his superior's eyebrows.

DRUNKS

- If you live in a dorm and one of your fellow housemates is one of those falling-down, obnoxious drunks who doesn't care that he wakes the whole house with his misbehavior, buy a couple of cans of extra-chunky cream of vegetable soup, mix them with a can of beer, and leave the slop to ripen in the sun for a couple of days. The next time your mark goes on a binge, wait till he makes it to his bed then drizzle your brew over the toilet and floor surrounding it. Smear a little of it on his sheets while you're at it. Your mark will be blamed for the mess, and, since he won't remember anyway, he will have to clean it up.

- If your mark likes to imbibe to the point of oblivion, yet still insists he's perfectly capable of driving, wait until he's found his way home and parked his car for the night. Then take an old shirt, lots of fake blood, and a plastic bag of chicken guts to adorn his car. Stick the bloodied shit to the grill after denting it a bit, and then splash the blood and guts all over the grill and hood of the car, making sure some gets on the windshield.

EARBENDERS

- Send salespeople (encyclopedia, cosmetic, vacuum cleaner, carpet, insurance, magazine, burial plot, correspondence school, interior decorators, religious proselytizers, roofers, painters, and other home-repair people, charity drive representatives and realtors) to your mark's home at inconvenient times.

ELECTRICAL

- Connect an on/off delay timer to an electrical circuit to either switch the circuit on or off at a preset time. Use this to engage auto-pilot in a private plane. Set it for several seconds or several minutes . . . just enough time for your dirty pilot target to dirty his pilot pants. These switches can be connected to automobile electrical systems, boats, motorcycles, and the overhead light bar of emergency vehicles, to name just a few.
- Select a wall-switch-operated electrical appliance (e.g., table lamp, TV set, stereo) in your mark's home. Make sure the power switch is off and then pull out the appliance's plug from the wall receptacle. Take a steel paper clip and place each end of the clip over the two prongs on the appliance's male plug. Slide the steel paper clip down to the base of the plug. Plug the appliance back in,

but do *not* turn on the power; leave that for your mark. When she hits the power switch, a violently major short circuit will take place, and all sorts of things will blow out.

ELEVATORS

- Have a female accomplice wait for the target to get off work and then casually bump into him in a crowded elevator, "accidentally" spilling some cheap perfume on him and smudging her lipstick on his shirt collar during the bump. It will probably arouse suspicion in his wife. To ensure that it does, a few days later, place a pair of worn panties under the seat of his car and spray some of the same cheap perfume into the car's interior.
- Rewire the floor indicator buttons on an elevator in a busy target hotel.

EMPLOYER

- Write a confidential note tipping off the victim's boss that the victim has been saying derogatory and incriminating things about the boss.
- Send the victim's boss an anonymous letter saying you saw the victim trying to pick up girls at a local elementary school and thought the boss ought to know before the man gets arrested and shames the company.

Or tell him the victim has herpes III and could contaminate the whole office if he's allowed to use the commodes in the company bathrooms.

- If the victim calls in sick to work, call his boss a couple of hours later and say you saw the victim at the beach or at a movie.
- Place company-owned documents or materials in your victim's jacket pockets or in his car, and then tip off the boss that he's stealing from the company or spying for a competitor.
- While your mark is on vacation, pose as a relative and call his boss and report that he's been killed in an accident.
- Call the victim's boss and tell him you're with the collection department of a large store and have a bad check from the victim. Tell him you've been trying for a week to collect your money, but the victim has ignored your calls. Threaten court action if the check isn't picked up by 5 P.M. that day.
- Tell your mark's boss that your are with the personnel department of another firm and that he's applied for a job there. Ask the boss what sort of employee the victim is—whether he's reliable, trustworthy, and so on.
- Type up a brief note lambasting the victim's boss. Insert it in an envelope, and then address the envelope to the boss in the victim's own handwriting (you'll need a sample of his writing for this). If the boss gets mad enough, he'll try to match the handwriting to people he knows—and odds are he'll zero in on the victim.
- Call the victim's boss and in an official-sounding voice say you're verifying his employment. Give the impression, without actually saying so, that you're a probation officer and that the victim has been con-

victed of some unspeakable crime like child molestation.

- If the victim deals with the public (e.g., salesman or waiter) call his boss and complain that you were treated shabbily by him. Accuse the victim of being discourteous, incompetent, thieving, and so on. Get other people to call and complain about the same thing.

ENTERTAINMENT

- If your target is a music buff, find a way to access his tape collection and either erase the tapes with a magnet or tape over them.
- If you're tired of tall people or women with big hair spoiling your view at the movie theater, take along a small bottle of mineral water (or for different effects, vegetable soup, glue, or honey) and pour it over the seat in front of you.
- Use a syringe to inject a little plaster or car-body filler into your mark's tennis balls. Use just enough to form a marble-sized lump, and his balls will really be out of balance.
- If your mark is a golfer, substitute trick balls that refuse to roll straight or that explode or disintegrate on impact for some of his balls. Or fill up one of the holes on the course with something really nasty like dog poop or maggots and make sure you lose that hole.
- If your mark is a TV junkie with one of those satellite dish eyesores in his yard, throw a handful of cement into the central waveguide aperture to severely disrupt his viewing pleasure. Or paint the dish with stone-textured paint or use wire cutters on the mesh. During the holidays, decorate the dish for the occasion with a little metal tinsel.

ENVIRONMENTAL RAPISTS (DEVELOPERS, BIG REAL ESTATERS, GAS AND OIL DRILLERS, ETC.)

- Any time you see a survey stake, pull it out and fill in the hole so that another stake isn't easily put up again.
- Move survey stakes far enough so that a lawsuit against the developer could ensue.
- Pour three or four quarts of Karo syrup into the fuel tanks of heavy machinery. They will be out of commission until they have had more than a bit of maintenance.
- Cutting tools and wrenches can do lots of damage to transmission towers and power lines.
- Open the valve on fuel-storage tanks so that the contents run into a nearby stream or pond. Call the state officials (and a television reporter or two) and report the environmental unconsciousness of the gas company.
- Move "Underground Cable" markers used by power and phone companies to mark buried wires and leave the rest to the oil company's bulldozer.
- If you live close to where a gas well is being drilled, spray weed killer on your own crops within a 100-yard radius of the gas well, then raise hell with the state agricultural people, and submit the gas company a bill for crop damage.
- To disable heavy water tank trunks, strategically place some two-inch thick pieces of 12-inch board through which you have first pounded several 10-inch housing spikes.

EXPLOSIVES

- Put some feces (or paint, cheap perfume, acid . . .) into a large Baggie. Gently break the glass of a large wattage light bulb without disturbing the filament. Gently attach the filament to the fuse of an M80. Make sure the light switch is off, and then screw the bulb carefully back into a ceiling socket and move the bag of feces (or whatever) up and around the light fixture, making sure the fuse and filament do not touch the feces, but that the M80 does. Tape the bag to the ceiling. About four seconds after the light switch is turned on, the shit (or paint, cheap perfume, acid) will literally hit the fan (or the man).
- Sprinkle a cup of old-fashioned black powder around the bottom of your mark's barbecue grill, fireplace, woodstove, oven, etc. When the powder ignites there will be a large flash and a huge, white, smelly cloud of smoke.
- Make a smoke bomb by combining four parts sugar to six parts saltpeter. Heat the mixture over a low flame until it starts to gel into a plastic-like substance. Remove the goop from the heat and allow it to cool. As it is cooling but is still pliable, stick a few wooden match heads and a fuse into the mass. This device is nonexplosive and nonflammable, but a pound of it will make enough thick smoke to cover a city block.
- To (possibly literally) scare the shit out of your target, bundle a few red road flares together and wrap them with black plastic

tape. Connect your creation with some coiled wire to an old, ticking alarm clock and place it where your mark can't miss seeing and hearing it.

- If you just want to put a scare into your pushy, complaining feminist mark, when she's out of her office, use duct tape to secure a training grenade (empty and unarmed) under her desk and attach a trip wire to her chair. Add a typed note to the grenade reading, "Women ARE equal to men, but whiney, hypocritical bitches die faster."

EYEGLASSES

- If you have access to your mark's eyeglasses, take them to one of those eyeglasses-while-you-wait places and have different prescription lenses put in them.

FAST-FOOD STORES

- If you work in a fast-food establishment and are tired of demanding, obnoxious customers, pay them back by coughing up hawkers and blowing them into their food before serving it, dabbing little flecks of feces on their burgers after they're cooked, or peeing in the french fry grease.
- If you're ticked off at a fast-food establishment (and who wouldn't be after reading all the gross stuff they do to your food), pull up into its drive-through line and order a huge, expensive, and complicated meal, and then drive through the line and far, far away.

FEARS

- Everyone is afraid of something—odd noises at night, strange lights or sounds, bizarre telephone calls, cult and occult pictures sent through the mail, spiders, snakes, someone staring. Find out what bugs your mark and use the information wisely.

FEMINISTS

- The next time a feminist commando type gets in your face about how a woman can do anything a man can do, ask her to whiz in a long-neck bottle without a funnel.

FILLERS

- Super foam products, commonly used as fillers, are urethane and resin compounds, usually in a spray can, that billow out and expand into a mass at least 30 times their original volume. They harden quickly into a strong material that is water, erosion, and corrosion proof, and heat and cold resistant. These can be used to fill just about any space you care to imagine.

FIRE

- Replace the easily shattered glass in your mark's fire extinguisher with some un-breakable, plexiglass or bulletproof armored glass, then tip off the fire department and your mark's insurance company that your mark is about to set off an insurance fire and claim he couldn't get to his fire extinguisher.

FISH

- If your mark is a fish fanatic, slip a few Alka Seltzer in the tank.
- Add a couple of small water snakes to your mark's aquarium or hook up a current activator or submersible heater to your mark's room light switch and let them create their own school of electric eels.

FLOWERS

- If someone has been stealing the best flowers from your garden, rig the lushest flower stalks with a thin wire that leads to a capacitor and a relay that starts a tape player. Next time the flower rustler leans into the bed with her scissors, she'll get a slight electric shock from the capacitor and an even bigger shock when the flower hisses, "Get your thievin' hands off me!"
- If your mark is an arachnophobe, send her a lovely floral arrangement with a nice, hairy spider in it.
- If you've been left for another woman, send her a lovely bouquet in your ex's name, but include in it a couple of twists of poison ivy.

FLOWER SHOPS

- If you've ordered a bouquet to be sent sight unseen from a florist to a friend and it turned out to be sight that should have remained unseen, make a visit to the store and add a few drops of chemicals to the arrangements in the display window.
- Call and order flowers delivered to miscellaneous places and charge them to another of your enemies.
- Order 100 wreaths for graves on Memorial Day and give a fake credit card number.

FOOD

- Get a candy mold from a confectionery supply house in the form of a bunny or Christmas tree, or something festive. Melt a little bit of real chocolate and a good bit of chocolate laxative together and fill the mold. Leave your creation on your mark's desk

with an anonymous "thank-you for being such a nice friend" note.
- Carrying the practice of an eye for an eye to its ridiculous extreme, if you want to get classic revenge, collect fish or sea creature eyes and serve them to your mark with (or in) cocktails or cups of tea or coffee.
- If you're truly pissed off at someone, freeze some urine in ice cube trays and use them to chill her next Scotch on the rocks.
- Add maggots to ice cubes before you freeze them, and take an entire bag of doctored ice to your target's party and introduce them into the punch bowl.
- Pour a glass of milk under your target's couch cushions. Things will turn sour in a couple of days.
- Squeegee your mark's windows with condensed milk in the winter. It will be almost impossible to get off until the weather gets warmer.
- Exchange the paper labels from cans of dog food with those from cans of vegetables in your mark's pantry.
- Substitute sugar for salt, plaster of Paris for flour, engine oil for olive oil, or baking soda for coffee creamer in your target's cupboards.
- If your mark will be away for a few days in the summer, puncture the lids of the cans in his cupboard. By the time vacation is over, he'll have a real welcome-home surprise waiting for him.
- Hide a rotten potato in your mark's ventilation ducts or wedge one behind the pipes in the bathroom. If your mark is a co-worker, hide one in the back of her bottom file drawer where she never looks anyway. You say potato, I say potatOH!
- Put a carton of raw eggs in your mark's microwave, set it on high for two minutes, and use that time to skedaddle.
- Grind up some cat-worming pills in your parasite mark's spaghetti sauce (or some

other strong-flavored food to mask the flavor). The result will be nausea and a case of the green apple quickstep. Thatsa some spicy meatball!

- Add a few magic mushrooms to your mark's salad, soup, or casserole.
- If your target is a tea drinker and likes to leave those little wet tea bags lying around to dry, get some chewing tobacco that is sold in little bags. Now stick a few into your target's box of tea bags.
- Hide some unpopped popcorn in your mark's toaster, coffee maker, microwave, oven, or charcoal grill.
- Stick some unpopped popcorn kernels in your mark's hamburger patties or frankfurters just before a barbecue or add some to her eggs for a real scramble.
- Dump some unpopped corn in your target's clothes dryer.
- Add meat to your vegetarian mark's meal.

FORGERY

- Forged letterheads, documents, and official cables can thwart any number of your mark's best efforts.

FOREIGN OFFICIALS

- Send a package of banned books to a foreign official, but address the parcel to a department other than his own.
- Send postcards with cryptic messages on them to foreign officials. Say something like, "The sun is out, and the water is fine." Postcards are so darned tempting to read, and communist officials are sufficiently paranoid that such a message just might prompt an investigation into your mark's corruptibility.

FREELOADERS

- If your mark is unemployed and collecting compensation, call the unemployment office and report that he's making $500 a week painting houses and isn't reporting the income. He'll be quizzed and possibly investigated.

FUNERALS

- Get a female to call a local funeral home and say she wants to make funeral arrangements for her late husband, who was killed in a car accident in another city. Have her ask the parlor to send someone to discuss the arrangements with her. Give the victim's address.
- Phone the victim's obituary in to your local newspaper, following the format of an obituary actually in the paper. Say that you're from a local (name it) funeral home. Most newspapers take this kind of information over the phone without question.
- You could have some fun with your least favorite mark/preacher at a funeral by putting an inappropriate T-shirt on the deceased or a bumper sticker on the casket.

GADGETS AND DEVICES

- You could really ruin your old movie buff mark's day by stuffing something other than a videotape into the VCR's tape slot. A couple of poached eggs, doggy doo, a small magnet, superglue. You get the picture--but your mark won't.

- Attach a small piece of sticky tape to the recording head of your target's VCR. The tape will prevent electrical contact between the head and the videotape, so the screen will remain blank.

- If you can get hold of a really strong industrial magnet and have access to your target's television for about five minutes, you can really change her view on things. Turn the set on and place the magnet against the screen. The magnet interferes with the flow of electron particles in the picture tube and will eventually cause a black spot the size of the magnet to appear on the screen so the picture is permanently distorted. This is a good way to get back at an unscrupulous appliance store that sold you a lemon of a TV and refuses to do right by you. Just sneak the magnet into the store in a briefcase or purse and hit as many sets as you can.

- Reset the tracking on your target's VCR then superglue the knob in that position.

- If your want to disable your mark's stereo speakers, television, or amplifiers, simply pour some iron filings (or cut-up steel wool) into a flexible plastic straw, stick the straw through the ventilation spaces of the appliance (or into the magnet gap of the speakers), and blow.

- Shove a straight pin through the cord on one of your mark's electrical appliances. Using a pair of wire cutters, clip the protruding ends of the pin as close to the cord as possible so they can't be seen and plug the appliance back into the wall. Next time your mark turns the appliance on, the pin will create a short circuit between the wires. There will be an impressive flash and puff of smoke and a blown fuse. Your mark will probably just replace the fuse and try again, with the same results.

- To make your mark think his favorite appliance has seen its last, paint the prongs on the plug with several coats of clear nail polish. The polish will act as an insulator and prevent the current from getting through.

- Is your target one of those gossipmongers who doesn't care about truth as long as she has something to whisper about? Poke holes in the dustbag of her vacuum cleaner. Next time she vacuums, she'll see what spreading dirt is all about.

GARAGE SALES

- Have a garage sale in your mark's name, but

at his neighbor's address. List all kinds of amazing bargains like guns, old china, glassware, and antiques. Set the sale to begin at 8:00 A.M., and the first obnoxious participant will no doubt arrive at 6:00 A.M. in order to get a head start.

GARBAGE

- Send your mark a "notice" from his garbage-collection company saying his collection days are being changed. He'll put out his garbage only to have to retrieve it. When the collectors really do come, his garbage won't be out, and he'll be stuck with the smelly stuff for days.
- Write an angry letter from your mark to the garbage-collection company complaining that the workers on his route aren't picking up all the trash, are littering, are making passes at his wife, and so forth. The company's boss will chew out his crew, and, doubtless, they'll zero in on the "liar" on their route.

GASES

- Ammonium sulfide is cheap and smells so bad your dog will tuck his tail and run from it. It can be sprayed or vaporized, so it can be used in any number of circumstances . . . dinner parties, drive-in movies, through a bedroom window—use your imagination.
- A small uncapped bottle of butyric acid (really stinky stuff) can be propped near a door to be knocked over the next time someone enters the room.
- Spray cans of insecticide serve nicely as improvised defense weapons. Insecticide burns the eyes, and the cans will shoot an 8- to 10-foot spray.

GASOLINE

- Pour dissolved candle wax into your mark's gasoline supply. Running this mixture through his automobile, boat, tractor, snowmobile, or whatever will create all kinds of hell with filters, critical tolerances, and so on.

GATES

- Any time your mark's gate is closed, open it. His expensive pure-bred dog could get out and run away, or something undesirable could get in.

GENITALS

- Get your female mark worried about genital odor by sending her anonymous packages of feminine hygiene products with notes that say things like, "Thought you could use this," "Use these—protect the environment," and so on.
- Add spearmint oil to douching solutions, lubricators, or tampons, or lubricate condoms with it. When moisture activated, it heats up like a bonfire.
- Enlist the bartender at your mark's party to stand around scratching and rearranging his nuggets before he puts a handful of ice in the drinks. It might be a nice touch to have previously frozen a few trays of ice with coarse, curly hairs in each cube.

GIFTS

- Have a huge, expensive bouquet of roses delivered to the victim's wife. Charge them to him and have the card say, "Because I love you, Darling." The victim won't dare admit he didn't send them, and he'll have to pay for them. The next week send a similar bouquet and note to his secretary, ex-wife, or wife of his worst enemy. Have the bill and a copy of the note sent to his home.

- On the victim's birthday, send him a box of homemade chocolate chip cookies, in which you have substituted Ex-Lax for the chocolate chips.
- Send a gift-wrapped bottle of douche to your victim's place of employment with an enclosed card that reads: "Happy birthday—here's something you could really put to good use." Her fellow workers will no doubt gather around while she unwraps it.
- If your mark is in the hospital, send him a voodoo doll with a pin placed in the area of the problem. Just before the victim is released from the hospital, call a florist and have a funeral wreath sent to his home.
- If someone in your target's family has just passed on, send the target "wish you were here" cards from the deceased.
- If your mark is one of those people who will gladly accept a gift from anyone but doesn't believe in the courtesy of writing thank-you notes, write some on her behalf. Next time she has a birthday, find out who gave her gifts and send them each a note that says something like, "Thank you for the satisfactory gift. I will use it and think of you often, but can't help noticing that someone of your financial means and supposed good taste could have chosen a whole lot better gift and put out a little more of the green to ensure quality. But I do appreciate the gesture."

GOVERNMENT MAIL

- Get a batch of military recruiting material, address it to various individuals who would

be sure to inform the feds, enclosing personal or insulting notes with the mark's name and address intact, and then stuff them in those government envelopes that say, "Penalty for private use $300." Who knows, maybe the USPS is really serious about that message.

GRAFFITI

- Using a Magic Marker, write your target's spouse's first name, phone number, and a couple of kinky sex acts she is willing to perform on the walls in every rest room of every bar in town. Only the sleaziest of characters will ever call a number written on a rest room wall, but, hey, that's okay.
- Scrawl the victim's name and phone number on the bathroom walls of gay bars and indicate he's available to perform various sexual acts.
- Commercial graffiti (billboards and posters) can be used to announce your mark's emersion from the homosexual closet. They could boast a conservative political candidate's personal advocacy of gun control, gay rights, abortion, and so on.
- Bumper stickers (another form of commercial graffiti) can be used in a number of creative ways. Stick legitimate bumper stickers that champion your political candidate/mark to the painted rear surfaces of automobiles in a shopping mall lot. Have some bumper stickers printed up that say "Gay Is Great . . . Try It" and stick them on automobiles of bikers, right-wingers, clergy, and anyone else who feels threatened by homosexuals. Print up bumper stickers that say, "Honk if you're an asshole, too" and stick them on the cars of those you believe are deserving of the sentiment. "Ban Handguns" or "Hunt Hunters" bumper

stickers are great for redneck gun nuts. The list is only limited by your imagination.

GREED

- If your mark is a skinflint, braze a 20d nail to a 50-cent piece and drive it into a crack in the sidewalk. He'll probably lose his fingernails or maybe the blade of his favorite jackknife trying to get at the coin.
- Leave a wallet or purse tied to a black fish line in a road your target always travels while you hide in the ditch or bushes holding on to the other end of the string. When the target's vehicle screeches to a stop, pull the string and run.

GROSS MUSIC

- If your target prudette is having an afternoon tea with matrons of the higher side of society, liven up their party by arranging to have gross, ethnic, racial, or military music played over her expensive sound system. X-rated party records and explicit sex-sound recordings might really frost their crumpets.

GUESTS

- Had enough of that one person who always drops by unexpectedly about meal time and expects you to feed him? Keep a stack of dirty plates smeared with congealed gravy just for those occasions. Next time your guest arrives, just before serving the food, take one of the plates and hold it out for your dog to lick clean, explaining, "Sorry, I just haven't had time to do the dishes. So busy, you

know, but Slurpy here is one of the family, and he really does a number on a dirty plate." If this doesn't make your guest stop arriving uninvited, move, cause nothing will.

GUN CONTROL

- Put look-alike toy guns on the front seat of your gun-control fanatic mark's car, and then call the police and report a car with a handgun on the seat in plain view.
- Using a postal money order, get your mark a year's membership in the National Rifle Association.
- Pledge large sums of money in your mark's name to all of the "right to bear arms" groups.
- Attach bumper stickers to the rear decks of the vehicles parked at an antigun gathering. The stickers could read, "Support the NRA," "This Car Protected by Smith & Wesson," or "I Suck Gun Barrels."
- Find out the birthdays of your antigun target's kids. Then send them T-shirts bearing a picture of a sniper rifle with a caption that says things like, "Reach Out and Touch Someone," or enclose a shirt bearing the logo of a firearms manufacturer. The kids will really like the shirts and will raise hell if their folks try to stop them from wearing them.

GUN NUTS

- If your mark is an unscrupulous gun trader, fill a bottle with strong hydrochloric acid and leave it open in his shop just before it is closed for the weekend. When the owner opens up on Monday, every piece of iron in the shop will be covered with fine, red rust.
- If you can't get some hunter to kill bambis

somewhere other than on your property, get his license number and from that track down his name and address. Purchase some submachine gun parts, wrap them in heavy plastic, and bury them in his garden. Now report him to the BATF and the local police for trafficking in machine guns. Have the tip include some mention of the garden.

HALLOWEEN

If you're plagued by neighborhood bullies who come around after you are in bed and smash your carefully crafted jack-o'-lanterns, rig exploding devices for each pumpkin that will be activated when the pumpkin is picked up.

HAM RADIOS

- Get hold of some two-meter ham gear and a repeater guide from a ham shop and find an autopatch phone repeater in your area. This autopatch repeater will enable you to make free telephone calls 24 hours a day, using some fake call sign. Call your mark at inconvenient hours using this little arrangement. It can't be easily traced because it is a radio, but be careful: it can be traced directionally.

HAWKERS

- Hawkers are especially yukky specimens of phlegm that one hawks up from the nether regions of the throat and the waste canals of the nasal passages. Otherwise put, they are especially gooey masses of phlegm containing enough multicolored solids to make effective missiles. That

said, you could quietly deposit a few hawkers in the glassware at your target cafeteria or restaurant.
- If you have the guts and are faster than a speeding bullet, propel a hawker directly on your mark and skedaddle.

HIGHWAYS

- Substitute a road sign that reads "Gross Load Weight 15 Tons" for one on a bridge approach that reads "Gross Load Weight 5 Tons."
- Paint sawhorses to look like official blockades that are used to close highways, bridges, and so forth, and set them out in appropriate places.
- Place bogus "Detour" signs where they will be sure to play havoc with rush-hour traffic.
- To get back at county road crews that leave piles of debris in your driveway or block off the entry to your driveway with snow in winter, post some "Road Closed" or "Bridge Out" signs along the roads and bridges leading to your home.

HIJACKING

- Know a truck driver who is abusive to his wife on the few days he's home a week? Get him in a world of hurt by finding out where he's to pick up his next load for delivery, enlist the services of an accomplice accomplished semi driver, and get there before him. Identify yourself as the mark and spirit his load away. He'll have some explaining to do when he shows up at his delivery point with nothing but a load of feeble excuses.

HOLIDAYS

- Substitute fresh roadkill for the turkey at your mark's next Thanksgiving dinner.
- Invite every deprived/depraved minority to your mark's next holiday feast. They will appreciate her charity.
- Plant rotten Easter eggs around your mark's yard just before the big egg hunt.

HOMES

- If there is a mail slot on your mark's front door, hook his hose to the outdoor faucet, remove the power nozzle from the hose, insert the bare hose end through the mail slot and turn on the faucet. An alternative would be to release the contents of a fire extinguisher through the letter slot or a can or so of quick-drying expanding insulation foam.
- Time your indoor watering scam for when your target is going to be away for a few days and have ready a few pieces of moldy bread. Water your target's carpet thoroughly and leave the moldy bread on top. If it's warm enough, the mold should take hold, you'll leave your target with an interesting new color scheme on his carpet.
- Dampen your mark's carpet as described earlier and thickly scatter it with mustard and cress seeds. A couple of days is all that's needed for these hardy salad seeds to

sprout and take hold, turning the floor into a living green carpet that will be next to impossible to get rid of once it's taken root.
- Using a syringe filled with bleach, spell an appropriate message on your target's carpet.
- Add bleach to your target's carpet shampoo.
- Rake up a lawn bag full of pine needles and dump them on your mark's thick pile carpet.
- If your mark hates cats, some night scatter dead fish in obscure and unpleasant places around his home. If you want feline audio accompaniment, tie a large dead fish from a tree limb that is just out of the reach for the neighborhood cats, and as near to your mark's bedroom window as possible.
- Squirt liquid solder or superglue into your mark's door locks.
- Unplug your mark's freezer or turn it to defrost.
- Wrap roadkill in aluminum foil and stick it in your mark's freezer.
- Dump some fiberglass or insulation dust into the mark's washing machine. It will be picked up by the clothes (hopefully undergarments) and within half an hour of getting dressed, the person wearing the clothes will notice a terrible itching that will take two or three days to disappear. You might consider mixing the fiberglass or insulation dust with the mark's detergent powder for future anonymous attacks.
- If you can get to your mark's furnace, throw some sulfur in it. The rotten egg smell will linger in the house for a couple of days. If you want some fireworks to go along with this trick, throw in a mixture of potassium permanganate and sugar along with the sulfur.
- When you know your mark and family will be away for at least the weekend, hire a backhoe operator in your mark's name to come and excavate a hole in the yard in order to add a basement room. Stake out

the area to be excavated prior to the excavator's arrival. You, wearing a disguise, pose as the landscape contractor your mark "hired" to show the backhoe operator exactly where to dig. Tell him to bill the mark directly. Make sure you've rented a pickup truck, slathered its license plate with mud, and posted a bogus landscaping business sign on its door. After the digging has begun, leave to pick up your foreman and crew.

- Run a bead of superglue around the rubber door seal of your mark's refrigerator and around the cupboard doors.
- Fill hollow curtain rods in your mark's home with raw shrimp or slip a few of the little stinkers inside her removable sofa cushion covers.
- Saw the doorknob off your mark's front door and lightly epoxy it back in place so that it looks normal. A few twists of the handle and it will come off in your mark's hand.
- Set a bag of animal crap on your target's doorstep, set the bag on fire, ring the bell, and run like hell.
- If your target likes a nice fire on a winter evening, gain access to his roof and cover the chimney with some plastic garbage bags or a slab of rock or piece of metal. To make the smoke have a really foul odor, dump some sulfur over the logs in the grate before you seal the chimney.
- Get a bucket of pig's blood from a butcher (tell him it's for use in making homemade black pudding) and freeze it in ice cream containers or ice cube trays. Leave big blocks of blood in drawers, filing cabinets, or cupboards in your mark's home. Drop the cube-sized blood blocks all over the house to melt and leave a gory, smelly trail.
- Slip a pound of bait maggots, worms, or live

cockroaches into the foot of your target's bed and make sure the sheets are tucked in nice and tight.

- Substitute sliced cheese or lunch meat for bookmarks in your target's library.
- If your mark owns a large piece of wooded land, clear a small area in the deeper woods, add a fire pit, and a rough-hewn shack. Party there with some friends so the locale looks well used. Place stained underwear (including that of children) alcohol, and drug paraphernalia, plus literature and icons from the Klan, a satanist cult, voodoo, mutilated animal carcasses, porno pictures, and photo composites of local biggies around the area. Next call a local TV news station and say that you accidentally stumbled over this place while hunting. Then call the police.

HOOKERS

- Hire an "escort" to come to "your" house. Use your mark's name and one of her most upright, puritan neighbor's address.
- Pay a streetwalker with venereal disease to pick up your mark.
- Have your mark apply for a job as a Las Vegas hooker. Send an appropriate résumé and some "wow" pictures. If your mark is a male, have him suggest to the house that they become a full-service brothel. Have him say he swings both ways. Make sure to include your mark's address for the response.

HORSES

- You can lead a horse up a staircase, but it's hard as hell to get him to come down again. The same might be true of cattle, swine, sheep, goats, and so forth. Why not treat your mark to a long-lasting upstairs barnyard?

HOTELS, MOTELS, AND HIGH RISES

- If you are served a meal that is not to your liking at a hotel restaurant, and get snooty behavior but no satisfaction when you mention it to the manager, let the dust settle and then rent a deposit box in the hotel safe and deposit the offending slab of meat into it. In due time, the desk crew will be accosted by the not-so-pleasant odor of your decaying din-din.
- Carry the parts of a small automobile to your mark's room when you're sure she will be out for some time. In the room, reassemble and weld the pieces back together with a portable welder.
- Hide small dead things like mice and birds in out of the way places in your target's rented room. Hide them in light fixtures, inside switch boxes, in unused overcoat pockets, and inside appliances.
- Use a razor blade to cut a small hiding hole into the pages of the Gideon Bible in your target motel. Fill the hole with a packet of condoms along with a note "from" the motel management, written on a memo pad with the motel's logo. The note should tell the religious folks to use the rubbers to "get it up so they could get it on with a really religious experience." Sign it St. Peter, lay minister.

HOT TUBS

- Dump five pounds of fertilizer in a target

apartment's Jacuzzi. The vulgar smell will waft throughout the entire apartment complex.

HOUSES

- Call several real estate firms and tell them you want to list your house for sale. Give them your victim's name and address and invite them to come by in the evening. He will send away some angry real estate salespeople, but, a few days later, when you send letters of apology from your mark to each real estate company saying he's sorry about turning them away the first time and he's changed his mind and wants to list his house with them, the eager-for-listing beavers that they are, will be forgiving and will once again appear on his doorstep. After that dust has settled, place a newspaper ad saying the victim's house is "For Sale by Owner." Ask a ridiculously low sale price. Would-be bargain hunters will flock to his door, and, once again, so will some realtors, insisting he will get a higher price if he sells his house through them.
- Remove the rain gutters from your mark's home. When it rains, the water will end up in his basement.

HOUSE PLANTS

- Add food coloring to the water before you water your mark's favorite houseplants. The plants will develop colored "veins" running through the stems and leaves just before they bite the dust.

HUNTERS

- Arrange for your favorite hunter/mark to receive some custom-loaded shotgun shells. Instead of the usual shot, load the shells with a combination of corrosive salts, coarse sand, tiny lead balls covered with grinding compound, plus steel burrs. Use flammable padding instead of the normal plastic wadding. The special loads will do wonders for his shotgun, his psyche, and his budget.

HYPOCHONDRIACS

- If your mark is a hypochondriac, enlist some conspirators to keep him at the doctor's office instead of at work. One day have someone say he's looking pale and have someone else ask if he's feeling all right. Next time he coughs, spread the symptoms of a terrible virus around the office, indicating that it begins with a slight cough. A couple of days later, have someone comment that a mole he has looks just like the skin cancer her sister had.

ID CARDS

- If you know of a nasty cabby whose hobbies are lying, cheating, and stealing, make up a few new ID cards for him—you know, those official ID cards with photo and description that are put up facing the backseat. Borrow an original card blank from the issuing authority and design a series of creative cards. Substitute a picture of a person of a different race or gender for his photo, or put a name like Ho Chi Minh, or Al Capone on the card. Or use his real picture and name and write lines and messages like, "I eat pussy," "I kiss little boys," "I can see your snatch," or "I just ate a booger sandwich," in the description lines. Switch the cards periodically. He'll wonder why his tips are so low.

INFERIORITY COMPLEX

- If your victim has physical shortcomings that he's concerned about, make him even more conscious of them. If he's overweight, for example, cut out pictures of fat people, hippos, elephants, and pigs, and mail them to him. If he's going bald, send him brochures from hairpiece manufacturers.

INSURANCE

- Call all the insurance offices in town and tell them you're worried about leaving your family destitute in case you should suddenly die. Ask them to drop by your house and add, "I'm not home until 9 o'clock, but you're certainly welcome to drop by any time after that." Give them your victim's name and address.
- Make a mass distribution of a realistic-looking official state government document that "legalizes" nonpayment of insurance premiums and authorizes personal liability lawsuits against sales agents, claim settlers, and company officials. It will create temporary panic within the insurance industry.

INSURANCE COMPANIES

- To get back at insurance companies for all their junk mail hustles, answer their requests with affirmative orders. Then run salespeople and clerks through a few scheduled/broken/rescheduled/rebroken, appointments before finally actually keeping an appointment and settling on a policy. Then wait until at least the second billing to cancel to ensure that they go to the expense of preparing and processing the policy.

IRS

- Here's a chance to use the IRS to your advantage for once. Get hold of your mark's Social Security number, address, and phone number. Then call the regional IRS office and "confess" that you have cheated on your income tax, your conscience has bothered you, and you want to make things right. Make an appointment with an auditor. When the mark doesn't show up for the appointment, the IRS will send a visitor to talk with her and chances are she will be audited for good measure.

- You can hassle the IRS by picking up a bunch of blank returns and filing them in with the names of your least favorite people, your pets' names, or the names of fictional characters. Some bureaucrat will have to make an effort to verify each return.

- Call your victim posing as a Mr. Schwartz (or some such) with the Internal Revenue Service, saying that you are auditing his accounts for the year 1975. Ask him to please bring his records for that year to the IRS office at 8 A.M. the following day. Give him the actual address of the office.

JAIL

- If your are communicating with a prisoner via the mail and don't want your letters inspected by the officials in charge, send your correspondence in official-looking legal envelopes with a printed return address that reflects some official in the criminal justice system. Mark the outer and inner envelope "OFFICIAL/CONFIDENTIAL."
- Get hold of some fingerprint ink from the booking area and apply some to staff toilet seats, doorknobs, telephone receivers, and so on.
- If you know some bully who has finally been tossed in the clink for one of his many crimes against civilized people, make his stay interesting. Buy a cheap used gun and a box of shells at a flea market. Then disassemble the weapon and wrap it and the ammunition carefully. Mail it to the bully in jail, using the bully's kid brother's return address. If you don't like guns, mail a knife, drugs, or any other legal no-no.

JEWELRY

- Ever been duped into buying a "solid gold" chain or ring that turned out to be gold plated? Return to the store indicating how deliriously happy you are with the first piece and state that you want to buy about

a dozen more. Then, when all the items are in front of you, take out a container of potassium iodide (which will strip gold plate, but leave solid gold unharmed) and inform the jeweler that, just to be on the safe side, you are going to check that the items are all solid gold—and start dropping them in.

JOCKS

- If your mark plays baseball, drill out a bat as if to cork it, only fill the cavity with about three ounces of black powder, tamp it really well, and top with some match heads of the strike-anywhere variety. Seal the seam. If the mark connects solidly with a pitch anywhere near that seam, only God and the team laundry folks will know just how scary that trick can be.
- Muscle types who like to break things irritated you lately? If your mark breaks boards, reinforce them with metal rods or a coat of lacquer. Replace older, weaker bricks that Mr. Macho will crack with fireplace bricks. If your mark likes to break ice blocks for his macho act, he may cheat and salt the block first. Substitute sugar for his salt.

JOGGERS

- Arm yourself with boards, pies, or other

objects and toss them at joggers as you drive by, swerving to miss running them down.

- Reduce the size of tire spikes and drop them near or on a jogging path. They will penetrate the joggers' jogging shoes and possibly the joggers' jogging feet.
- Ultrathin piano wire strung shin-high on a pathway can be excruciatingly nasty.
- Sprinkle marbles on their jogging paths or put ground glass inside their running shoes.
- If you're a jogger who wants to get even with a nasty passer-by, mace is a good choice. You can also carry cans of gaudy-colored spray paint to direct at your attackers' automobiles.

JUNK MAIL

- Collect junk mail till you have a good stack of it (this shouldn't take long) and fill a couple of cardboard boxes with the stuff along with notes about how irritating it is to receive so much junk mail. Now take several of their postage-paid envelopes and stick them on the front of the boxes and junk-mail them back.
- Fill a box with rocks, sugar, or flour. Slap a junk mail postage-paid envelope on the box and send it to them. Enlist about 40 friends to do the same thing. Weighty message.
- Stuff prepaid envelopes with pornographic pictures and send them back to the companies' headquarters.
- Collect a bag full of your target's junk mail, then take it to a park and dump it. Then call the authorities, telling them you saw someone littering in the park, and, as a concerned citizen, you thought someone ought to know.

KIDDIES

- Buy your mark's kids a loud musical instrument, such as drums or an electric guitar.
- Send your mark's little ones explicit porno in the name of some secondary mark.
- Send your mark's children unusual pets for their birthdays and holidays. Geese, porcupines, skunks, or a pair of mating rabbits might be nice.

LANDLORDS

- If you have been evicted unfairly from your apartment, get back at your landlord by arranging to sublet the place to a group of undesirables (drug addicts, drunks, prostitutes, bikers).
- Pay a nasty landlady back for an unfair eviction by leaving behind a garbage can full of fish placed strategically where the sun always shines.
- If your landlord or landlady seems set on confining your behavior in accordance with her narrow definition of moral, a few periodic, well-positioned window signs ("For a good lay call [fill in a name]," "[Fill in a name] is gay," "[Fill in a name] likes S&M," "Whorehouse under new management") might cause her to be so concerned about her own moral business that she will forget to put her nose into yours.

- If you've suffered at the hands of a lax landlord and are about to leave his life for good, buy a few bags of sugar, turn off the electricity supply to the apartment, unscrew the light-switch plates, and, using a small funnel, pour a good amount of sugar into each wall cavity. You can purchase some cockroaches from reptile food suppliers and funnel them through the holes after the sugar. Then replace the switch plates and turn the electricity back on.
- Drop raw chicken legs down the wiring holes of your apartment just before you leave. The smell won't become really foul for a couple of days. Dead mice and fish heads do nicely too.
- Paint a liberal coating of hydrochloric acid on the lead seal of the water pipes in your apartment just before you move out. That will leave the pipes and your landlord fit to burst.
- If your landlady refuses to call in an exterminator for your apartment to get rid of cockroaches and such, get some termite eggs from a science supply house and plant them in the mark's house. If the landlady lives in the same building as you do, you might want to use the termites' gestation period to find another apartment.
- "Borrow" a bicycle from another tenant and place it on the landlord's balcony. The other tenant will make a stolen bicycle report and when the police question the landlord about

how and why the bike got on his balcony, his explanation will be, shall we say, less than believable.

- Print up some official looking NOTICE OF ENTRY door hangers that read as follows: "ON_____, I_____ entered your residence for the official purpose of _____." Fill in the date, the landlord's name, and then write various purposes on various hangers and attach them to tenants' doors in random fashion. Some of the purposes could include TO STEAL, TO MASTURBATE IN YOUR MILK, TO TAKE A SHIT, TO WEAR YOUR WIFE'S UNDERWEAR, TO FANTASIZE ABOUT MAKING LOVE TO YOUR CHILD.

LAND RAPISTS

- Bury ssuch objects as arrowheads, odd pottery shards, or human skulls snitched from a bio classroom in an area where a developer is about to develop. Tip off some anthropology students who like to work on digs, and let them discover your "artifacts." Insist through the local historical society that moral and legal pressure be brought to bear on the developer to halt his operations until a scientific dig can verify the findings.
- Load several pickup trucks with garbage bags filled with Styrofoam peanuts. On a dark and windy night, go to the building site and open the bags and let nature and the peanuts help you pay back the bastard who messed up the real landscape. Those peanuts can't be raked up or sucked up with a commercial vacuum. They have to be picked up one at a time.
- Acetylene grenades will disable large yellow machines. Fill a small balloon with the product and introduce it into the air cleaner

assembly of a diesel engine. When the engine is started, the balloon and its contents are sucked into the induction system. The fuel ignites prematurely and could break a piston rod.

LAUNDROMATS

- Dump several packets of dye into your mark's wash. If you do this at random in a Laundromat, the owners will suffer some grief.
- Put small piles of moistened rust particles in the dryer used by your mark so the mark's clothing will have large rust stains when it's removed from the dryer.
- Many additives make for good fun at a Laundromat, including raw eggs, fish, peanut butter, chewing gum, and fiberglass.
- If your mark is the Laundromat operator, bugger ancillary services like vending machines, customer seats, and rest rooms. Small nails or staples driven partly into chairs will snag customers' clothes. Jam coin slots in vending machines with slugs, glue, or whatever you have handy. Customers complain when they can't pass the time with a bottle of soda and a box of Jujubes.
- If you've had coins ripped off at public laundries or clothes torn in their machines, throw a couple of cheese slices into one of the dryers. Set the machine to "hot" and "cook" for about 10 minutes.
- If your target uses a public laundry, wait until he puts his loads in and runs across the street to get a cup of coffee while he waits. Then add bleach or acid to his fabric softener or mix dye into his powdered detergent.
- Take crayon pieces and scatter them inside a dryer drum where there are lots of holes. The sheets come out looking tie-dyed.

- If you're seeing red because you're having trouble with those slobs who remove your clothes from the washer or dryer and substitute their own, add some red food coloring and beef bouillon cubes to the machines they stole.

LAWNS AND GARDENS

- Pour quantities of tomcat lure on the targeted lawn. It will do wonders for the lawn and the mark's disposition.
- Use a concentrated weed killer, salt, or vinegar to write socially offensive words on your mark's lawn. The grass will die, but the legend will live on.
- Use commercial defoliants to remove everything that grows on the lawns of marks who have unreasonable pride in their lawns and ornamentals. Make sure the label says the product is nonselective or that it makes the soil barren, load up your sprayer, stand upwind, and spray away.
- If your mark has a tendency toward paranoia and has a natural or LP gas meter, apply the defoliant fairly heavily around the meter and a little more lightly following the fuel line directly to the house. A final, heavier dose should be sprayed at the jointure of the home and line. In a couple of days, your mark will be convinced his entire gas system is leaking badly.
- Spray defoliant around your mark's house. Then on "official" letterhead, send the mark a letter from the Nuclear Regulatory Commission explaining that it's just discovered some records indicating that the mark's home was built over a former nuclear waste repository. Don't use this if the mark's house was built before 1960, because nuclear waste dumps weren't built much before then.
- When the mark and his family leave town, call a landscaping firm or tree surgeon and tell them to remove a large tree from his yard, explaining that it is diseased or is blocking your view. Or send over a lawn service to cut his grass, trim his hedges, and send him a big bill. Or pay for a truckload of gravel or lumber and have it dumped in the victim's garden, lawn, front porch.
- Order a load of manure in your victim's name. While he is at work, have it spread on his front yard, explaining that you plan to use it as fertilizer.
- Visit your mark's property late at night and carefully cut a groove around each of her trees and bushes with a pocketknife. This will cause them to die and cost her a fortune to replace.
- If your target is a gardener, plant weed seeds right behind her vegetable or flower seeds. Or plant marijuana seeds on her back lot and call the authorities.
- To kill a tree or a limb of a tree, cut through the cambium layer with piano wire, or pound copper nails into the trunk.
- Spray paint your mark's lawn in your favorite shade in the middle of the night, using a rented backpack spray device.
- Pour liquid laundry detergent or cornflakes all over your target's lawn just before a rainstorm.
- Break into your target's shed or greenhouse and substitute weed killer for insecticide or plant food.
- Every time you drive by your mark's lawn, throw a stone in it. It'll do wonders for his power lawn mower.
- If your mark is gullible or a patriotic sap, dump an exceedingly large, cumbersome,

ugly, and odd-shaped piece of concrete on his property or lawn. Have affixed to it an authentic-looking metal label that reads, "U.S. Government Time Capsule—Do Not Remove Under Penalty of Federal Law. U.S. Department of the Interior." Bureaucratic shuffling of paper and arguments over just whose jurisdiction it really is could slow up resolution of the problem. Stuff like this is big news to small newspaper and radio and TV stations.

- Passion fruit, blackberry, and trumpet creeper are fun to plant on your mark's lawn whilst said mark is away for a couple of weeks. These invasive plants are almost impossible to get rid of once started.

LAWSUITS

- Law libraries have all the legal forms and information necessary to sue someone. Clerks can even be asked for help. With this in mind, why not just sue your mark for damages done, mental anguish, being such a jerk . . .

LAWYERS

- To get back at a shyster who is attempting to become a politician, duplicate his legal letterhead and send out blatant letters over his signature demanding campaign contributions from politically sensitive people, or send threatening letters to local civic, church, and charity groups concerning their illegal bingo and 50/50 fund-raisers. Have your lawyer mark threaten legal action.
- If you have access to a law library, copy some standardized legal practice forms from books and routine stationery forms that

lawyers, clerks, and judges use to help draft legal letters and proper legal forms. A dummy form or letter, Photostatted with some dummy legal notices, using, for example, arrest warrants, summonses, condemnations, search warrants, and so on, can often pass for the real thing. They will easily fool your target and will probably force his or her attorney to at least follow up on the problem . . . for a modest fee, of course.

LIBRARIES

- Ever been charged by a library for a lost book that you are certain you returned? Spend a few dollars and have some book title plates printed. They are those snobbish gum-backed labels that announce a book's title, author, and donor. Fill them in with your most creative pornographic, bogus information and paste them in the old classics at your target library.

LICENSE PLATES

- Remove your mark's license plates when he's planning to be in a bar for a couple of hours. When he leaves the bar to drive home, the police will likely stop him for the missing plates, smell the booze on his breath, and ask for a little roadside demonstration. With any luck, your mark won't pass the test.
- You can alter the numbers on license plates with a little same-color paint and just a few strokes of a paintbrush. Stick to ones that are easy, like changing a 3 or a 0 to an 8, a 1 to a 4 or a 7, and so on. When your mark drives off, report the car stolen and give the altered plate number.

LOCKS

- Stick a toothpick in the lock of the trunk of your victim's car and break it off. He'll eventually have a flat tire and won't be able to get his spare out of the trunk. You can also plug up his car door locks this way.
- Jimmy open a school bully's hall locker and lard it with some drug- and porn-related contraband, and then relock the thing with the same school-issue combination lock. Paint over the raised white numbers with heavy black paint so, when he comes back to open his locker, the idiot will have to call a custodian over to open the lock. The custodian will likely later involve the principal, the parents, and the police.
- Roll a tiny piece of aluminum foil into a thin sliver. Push this sliver into the keyhole of your mark's lock with a toothpick. When the mark inserts the key, it will push the foil the rest of the way in, and it will seem as if the key is home. But no matter how much he twists and turns, the lock just won't open. An expensive lock will cost your mark a pretty penny to get fixed.

LUGGAGE AND BRIEFCASES

- Use a nail gun to shoot and fasten your mark's luggage or briefcase securely to a cement slab floor. Or if you can guarantee an overnight setting time, use one of the many (quieter) epoxy products to serve the same purpose.

LUNCH BOXES

- If you have a problem with someone at work pilfering lunches out of the community refrigerator, sprinkle some yellow phenolphthalein crystals (makes ya poop) on a couple of lunches and leave them in the refrigerator.
- Clip some disgusting porno pictures, or get a bogus love letter written to the mark, or select some used rubbers or sexy underpants, and plant them in your mark's lunch box after he's done with it for the day. The fun begins when his wife opens the box at home that night to clean it out for the next day.

MA BELL

- Overpay your telephone bill by 17 cents a month for a few months and then underpay by 17 cents for the same number of months. Start another pattern of consistent over-payment and underpayment. It will drive the bookkeepers nuts.
- Hang "Out of Order" signs with the local Ma Bell's logo on them on every public telephone you can find.
- From a pay phone, order phones and equipment for your marks or ask that their service be cut off.
- To cause a little trouble at a company that does the majority of its business by phone, cut the female end off an ordinary extension cord. Next, unscrew the mouthpiece on the tele-phone in any office. There you will see a terminal for a red wire and one for a black wire. Attach one of the wires from the extension cord to the red terminal and one to the black. Finally, plug the extension cord into a power socket. This will send 120 volts of electricity back through equipment designed for 6 volts, knocking out numerous other telephones and the main switchboard.
- If your mark will be away for a few days, use call-forwarding to divert his calls to Moscow, Bangkok, or Perth. The mark will be billed for all the call-diversion services, international as well as national.

MAFIA

- If you're the female boss of a male employee who refuses to take instructions from a woman and continually makes comments about what you probably had to do to secure such a high-ranking job, make a phone call to a "mobster" friend, when your mark is within earshot. Make comments in whispers loud enough for the problem boy to hear about needing some "contract work done." Then purposely notice that he is listening and say quickly, "Can't talk now," and hang up. This plants the seed of paranoia. Then enlist a couple of burly actors to dress the part of a couple of hit men. Have them call on the troublemaker in his apartment, at his favorite bar, and in the company parking lot. Have them tell him he is an unimportant worm that nobody will miss and that he has two weeks to get a new job and get out of town.

MAGAZINE SUBSCRIPTIONS

- Subscribe to a homosexual magazine in your mark's name. Have it delivered to his place of business.
- Gather up every order form from every magazine in your local library. You will have well over a hundred magazine

subscription application forms on postcards with no postage necessary. Fill these out with your mark's name and address, check the box that says "To be billed later," and mail them a few at a time from several post offices so as not to draw attention to your act.

- To get back at those magazine distributors who advertise a free sample copy with no obligation to buy but who nevertheless continue to send you magazines and associated bills, collect a bunch of their order forms and send them in with phony names and addresses. Now let them try to collect.

MAIL

- Send single-entendre post cards bearing personal/sexual/medical messages to your mark's home.
- Posing as a medical researcher, con some crab lice eggs from a supply house. Insert the eggs with an innocuous business letter into an envelope addressed personally to your mark. When the mark opens and unfolds the letter, the lice eggs will drop onto his clothing and the surrounding area. You can use this same tactic but substitute itching powder, sneezing powder, or chemical tear gas powder for the lice eggs.
- Cut a large eye out of a magazine, paste it onto a sheet of paper, and mail it to your victim to serve as the first hint someone is watching him.
- Fill out a change-of-address form in your mark's name.
- Send your victim mail that says things like "I'll be in town on July 2. Will contact you. Very important." Leave the letters unsigned.
- Send a sexually suggestive letter to a bogus lady in (nonexistent) Kingstown, Tennessee,

making sure to put the victim's return address on the label.

- Mail the victim's wife a pair of sequined high heels with a letter typed on motel stationery that says: "Dear Mrs. _____, When you and your husband were here, you left these shoes in your room. We tried to reach you by phone but couldn't, so we have mailed the shoes instead. Please reimburse in the amount of $___ for mailing costs. Yours truly, Howard Colson, desk clerk."
- Type the mark's name and address on mailing labels, stick them on the sleaziest porno magazines you can find, and mail them to his home. More than likely, his wife brings in the mail.
- Send the victim's spouse an anonymous letter indicating that she is having an affair with an attractive office colleague.
- Write the victim a note on stationery from a motel known to rent rooms by the hour, asking that he return the key to room 117.
- Using your mark's letterhead, write to government officials and other people in the public eye demanding ridiculous things. Write the local newspaper in support of anything your mark is outspoken against.
- Whenever you get one of those unwanted, "work on your guilt button" mail solicitations for money, making sure you use their postage-paid envelope, send them some money—Monopoly or other play money.
- On official letterhead, say, for example, from the IRS, send your target partial letters. That is, send them only the "second page" of a letter with just a line or two of type at the top saying something in a threatening tone, like, "If you do not comply immediately with this directive, we will be forced to take matters further."

- If you have a need to get into a sealed envelope surreptitiously, wet the sealed flap portion, then nuke the missive in a microwave for 30 seconds at medium high. It will steam open the letter. Add live insects to the envelope, reseal it, and leave it for your mark to reopen.
- Send your mark a piece of sandpaper, one old glove, haircut detritus, half an old necktie, a diaper, an oddball, an obscure church bulletin. This sort of thing worries people.

MAILBOXES

- If your target has an especially unique mailbox, remove it under cover of night. Leave an official-looking notice along the lines of "Your mailbox has been removed by order of the Postmaster General in compliance with postal regulation P/B5526. Please contact your local post office for further instructions."
- Decorate your mark's mailbox with bird feathers and glue or put something inside— dog turds, toads, mice, rats, a mousetrap . . . use your imagination . . . ask yourself, is it smaller than a mailbox?
- Fill your mark's mailbox with nonvenomous snakes after the mail has been delivered.
- If your mark has an annoying cat that seems to prefer your yard to dump in, capture the kitty and dump it into the owner's mailbox.
- A bunch of ice cubes tossed into a mailbox or newspaper delivery tube on a warm day will make your mark's reading very soggy.

MALLS

- You know those peabrains who park their expensive cars in mall parking lots at an angle over several spaces to keep others from parking too close? Next time, park a car that you don't care much about at the same angle about 4 inches from the other car's driver side door, blocking entry for the asshole driver.
- How about the cretin who blocks the entrance to a crowded parking lot lane waiting for the next available space close to the mall? Simply drive up the next lane, then back down in front of the cretin and take the next spot yourself.
- If your mark plays a mall Santa, intercept some of the real notes that Santa's helpers write to tell what each kiddie wants for Christmas, and exchange them for some of your own, requesting sex toys, telling him to fondle the child, or stating that the child's parent wants to perform a bizarre sex act with Santa.

MANNEQUINS

- Attend a going-out-of-business sale and buy the store mannequins. Dress them in Salvation Army clothing or leave them naked if it would benefit your mission. Place mannequins on your mark's lawn, in his car, and in the hallway outside of his office. Mutilate the genital areas and write voodoo symbols and occult signs on the bodies using runny red paint for bloody look-alikes. Make their faces look like your mark and his family.

MARRIAGE

- Arrange an entire wedding for your mark— church, reception hall, caterer, and an orchestra, and send out invitations, having everything billed to your mark. Everyone will show up for the ceremony except the bride and groom. Guest will be miffed and merchants and other service providers will want to be paid for goods and services.

- Hire a bedraggled lady and child to troop into the reception and confront the groom/mark with the question of his continued child-support payments.
- Hire a gorgeous, lusty, sensually costumed woman to vamp up to the groom/mark at the reception and plant a deep wet kiss on him while cooing, "Don't forget our past, love. When you're tired of that little girl next door, you know where to find me." As she leaves, have her say, "Last week was tremendous. Don't be a stranger, a man like you needs a woman like me."
- Call the church office before the ceremony and say that a crazed ex-lover of the bride plans to destroy the reception. Just as the reception begins, arrange to have a bunch of M80s set off.
- Use additives in the punch and food.
- Hire someone (preferably a member of the wedding party) to vomit during the ceremony or the reception.
- Hire someone to slowly and dramatically flash the minister or singer from the back of the church while everyone else is facing front.
- Call the state police or the DEA and give them a complete description of the honeymoon car. Report that the couple are drug couriers disguised as newlyweds.

MASS TRANSIT

- One of the best ways to attack a bus or airliner is to gross people out. The simplest way is to vomit in such a way that the other passengers can't escape seeing or hearing your act.
- A large bag full of bees, horseflies, moths, or crickets placed open on a seat of a bus or train will do wonders for the morale of the passengers.
- Squirt some tear gas on a bus or train.

MEDIA

- Take or phone in a fake wedding story, being sure to give them a legitimate-looking bride/groom photo. Most smaller and medium-sized papers will publish without checking, which could lead to all sorts of wonderful things if you've been inventive in your choice of marriage partners.
- Use a low-power mobile transmitter to add little bits of original (obscene) programming to your community's commercial radio station.
- Insert paper-destroying insects or chemicals into rolls of newsprint at the local newspaper.
- Small radio stations are often staffed at night by just the on-duty DJ, who will eventually have to take a bathroom break. Wait until then and have an accomplice distract the DJ while you place a prerecorded cassette message of your own on the air.
- Phone a radio talk show and speak out on a controversial subject, choosing the least popular side and give your mark's name and address.
- Call a radio station and have them run a saturation campaign of 25 spots per day listing your mark and his home address and telephone number as a new pizza parlor. Advertise all sorts of promotional goodies like free delivery, free sodas, free extra cheese and sauce to the first thousand customers, and so on. The station will run

the ads a day or so before your mark can get them stopped.

- Call in and order a newspaper (magazine, trade publication) subscription in your mark's name and address. Then call your mark using the real circulation manager's name and tell him you are with the circulation department and that they're going to give you a free, trial subscription. When the papers start to arrive, the mark will think they're free. The fireworks begin when the bill arrives and your mark calls to complain.

- Call a radio station and report that your daughter has lost her beloved dog. Ask the station to broadcast a description of the animal and the fact that you are offering a $50 reward for its return. Give a vague description that could match just about any stray dog and ask that anyone finding the animal bring it to your home, using the victim's address, of course.

- If you live in a small town, call in requests for sappy songs with sappy dedications for your mark's spouse from his lover. In a small town, there are few secrets and lots of rumors.

- If a local newspaper refuses to run your letter or ad, go to a print-it-yourself shop and publish it as a one-page flyer. Then simply insert your addition into copies of the paper at local convenience stores and newsstands. If asked what you're doing, tell them it is a forgotten insert you need to add. Maybe they'll even help you.

MEDICAL

- Obtain some real medical test report forms from a hospital, clinic, or laboratory, or have a trusted printer make some for you. You will also need matching return-address business envelopes in which to mail the reports to your mark. Using medical textbooks or a trusted friend with a medical background as a guide, prepare a series of embarrassing lab reports for your mark (e.g., positive identification of venereal disease, drug dependence, AIDS, yeast infection, mental illness). Coordinate the mailing of the bogus report with a telephone call to the mark's spouse, employer, parents, parole officer. Mail appropriate duplicate copies of diagnostic reports to public health officials, state narcotics bureau, and so on.

- To really put your mark in the hot seat, remove some Preparation H from the container in his medicine chest and refill it with Tabasco Sauce.

- If you've been the victim of a nasty hospital nurse, fill an air-tight bag with animal crap and put it in a box that you wrap with bright Christmas wrapping paper. Enclose a personal note that says, "Just returning a little of what you are so fond of dishing out," and sign it "A former inmate." Mail the package to the nurse in care of the hospital, where she is sure to open it in front of her colleagues and maybe other patients.

- Leave dead vermin at strategic points of a medical facility that has caused you grief. Good spots are near the coffee shop, the kitchen, the emergency room, visitors' lounge, and so on.

- Dressed in whites or other appropriately colored uniform, slip in with cafeteria or kitchen help and put some harmless food coloring into foods. Or if you can get into where the staff food is prepared, add more powerful additives to the food.

- Get hold of some other person's medical insurance identification and use it to charge medical bills. The bills will be sent to a totally innocent or unaware third party who will, of course, be outraged about the whole business and refuse to pay.

MEGGER

- A megger is a really useful way to "smoke" such major electrical appliances as refrigerators, washers, dryers, and freezers. Electricians call this device a voltage generator or, in jargon, a megger. It's a hand-cranked device available from tool shops and electrical supply outlets, or you can rent one. A megger can produce up to 1,000-volt output, which can fry most appliances, especially the capacitor on a starter motor. Attach the AC line cord of your mark's appliance(s) to the megger and crank away your frustrations.

MEMORANDA

- Let's say your mark has been shafting you during the interoffice status rivalry game or taking credit for your good ideas or blaming you for her duds. You might want to intercept one of your mark's memos before it goes out, hold it a day, and then send it back with some horrible message scrawled on it next to some honcho's initials. Or you may want to destroy your mark's outgoing memos or the response memos, or cause copies of sensitive memos to go to the wrong people.

MICROWAVES

- Place a small piece of aluminum foil inside your target's microwave oven. Next time he turns it on, his machine will get zapped. Big surprises sometimes do come in little packages.

MILITARY

- Rent and wear a replica of a military uniform (wearing a real one is against the law) and give speeches, shout orders, make bogus policy pronouncements, hold press conferences, use rank, and all sorts of other bits of theater from which the average citizen might infer you really do represent the official military. This could cause all sorts of public relations and other problems for the military establishment.
- Find a somewhat deserted area of a large public park and put some official-looking, commercially printed signs in prominent places that say: "CAUTION—WARNING: Army war dogs training in this area. Very dangerous. Keep all children and pets within sight. If Army dog approaches, do *not* move under any circumstances." Brass hats will roll when frightened citizens complain.
- Send especially obnoxious recruits, second lieutenants, and other lower-order sorts on fool's errands for items such as a rubber flag to be flown on rainy days, a five-gallon drum of prop wash, a bucket of prop pitch, a box of RPMs, stuffing for the crow's nest, some dotted ink, or a can of plaid paint.
- If you have access to the sound system over which reveille is played each morning, move up the time it's played by half an hour. The next day, make it 15 minutes late. Another day, play it in the middle of the night.
- To get even with the selective service system or a particular military board, register yourself in about three dozen locations with an equal number of draft boards.

- Register legions of phantom people for service, using phony names and addresses.
- Just before inspection, introduce food that you've stolen from the chow hall into the mark's footlocker. Be sure it is covered, of course, and crudely.
- Request a transfer for your mark to some awful duty station. It won't go through, but an investigation will occur and your mark will be a major part of it, and he'll probably be marked as a troublemaker.

MIND AND EGO BUSTERS

- Select a magazine with a large picture of a face on the cover. Burn out just the eyes and the mouth and mail the magazine to your mark. Do this several times a month at random periods. It's a very eerie experience.
- Mail a sympathy card to your mark's wife. Inside the card, write a personal message, "So terribly sorry to hear about your husband's untimely death." Date the message two weeks in the future and mail it that day.

MINORITIES

- If your victim is a member of a minority or has an accent, report her to the immigration and naturalization office as an illegal alien.

MONEY

- Write your target's personal details on every piece of paper money you can get your hands on. List his name, address, home and work phone numbers, credit card numbers,

Social Security number, and so on, in hopes the information falls into the wrong hands.
- Write your mark's name address and phone number on paper money and advertise unusual sexual services on her behalf. The money will stay in circulation long enough for loads of sleazy people to get their hands on it.

MOONING

- When some prominent mark dies and it gets TV coverage, be sure to moon the funeral ceremony in the semidistant background just when and where the cameras are rolling.
- Seek out some cult religious organization with a gathering or some uptight graduation ceremony. Moon it.

MORAL SPHINCTER MUSCLES

- If some majestical majority goes into your community library and bans books at will, defacing and destroying books their mind-masters told them to waste, go to their library and deface, ruin, and destroy their books, using the same logic.

MOTION PICTURES

- If a theater employee offends you, return the next evening with several jars of huge moths. When the feature begins, release the creatures. They will all fly directly into the beam of the projector and stay and stay and stay.
- If you have ever suffered damages in a

movie theater (staining your clothes on some candy or gum some previous patron left on the seat, torn your pants on a spring protruding from a theater seat, or had butter from a popcorn tub ruin a perfectly good dress), and the management refused to pay any claims, you can get revenge. Just make sure you have a quick, clear exit. Take a container of lukewarm vegetable soup into the movie theater and sit in the balcony. Make the sounds of throwing up and dump the soup on the people below. The point is to have dozens of irate patrons demanding damage settlements from the management of the establishment.

MUNICIPAL SERVICES

- If you want to pay back a municipality for parking corruption, a squirt or two of concentrated battery acid or epoxy glue into a parking meter slot might give you some satisfaction. You can also insert small washers coated with liquid solder or glue into the meter slot.
- Set up a few sawhorses and some official-looking signs on a busy street just before rush hour.

- If you have a beef with a badass cop (leave the good ones alone) chain his black 'n white to the car parked behind it or to something that will cause a little damage, while he's in having a cup of coffee and a donut.
- Call the parents of kids who get into trouble and threaten them and their kids, identifying yourself as "Officer (your mark's name)."0
- If you see your policeman mark drinking in a public bar, make some "drunken"0 phone calls to some single and married women, using his name. Mention the name of the bar the mark is at and ask them to join you. Tell them you saw them and fell in love with them and let them know what a great lover you are. Get graphic, be boastful, make officially backed demands. If a husband or lover comes on the line, be verbally abusive and drunkenly threatening.

MUSIC

- Lock the transport device on the mark's turntable or laser disc player.
- Remove your mark's turntable needles; replace with nails.
- Cover your mark's VCR or audio deck heads with clear nail polish.

NEIGHBORHOOD

- If your mark is a bigot and lives in a neighborhood of like-minded rednecks, posing as the mark, set up an appointment to sell your house with a real estate salesperson who works for an agency that deals mostly with Blacks or Chicanos. You have given your mark's name, but you give the address of your mark's most ruby-necked neighbor.

NEIGHBORS

- Got a beef with your neighbors? Next time they put their trash out for pickup, liberally cover the bags or cans with hamburger grease or bacon fat. All the neighborhood animals will take this as a personal invitation, and they'll come over and rip into the garbage, searching madly for the elusive aromatic morsel. And we all know animals have a nasty habit of not picking up after themselves.
- Add a little trash to your neighbor's garbage, like porn magazines, exotic underwear, chains, and empty syringes. Then, making sure there's an envelope or two addressed to your target mixed in with the trash, dump it in other neighbors' gardens, on their doorsteps, and so on. A quick and easy way to trash a reputation.
- Anytime you're visited by salespeople, religious proselytizers, people seeking to do odd jobs, real estate agents, people asking for donations, and so on, tell them you're not interested but that you thought you heard your neighbor expressing some interest.
- Call the gas company on your target's behalf to report a gas leak at 3 A.M. Repeat off and on for a couple of months.
- Toss handfuls of leaf lettuce seeds all over your neighbor's lawn just before a heavy rain. It grows easily. Everyone needs a little roughage now and then.
- On a Friday night, unscrew your neighbor mark's cable TV hookup outside the house just enough to break the connection. Early Monday morning tighten it again. The cable company will come out, check it all, demonstrate that it is working, bill them for a service call, and leave. Repeat as necessary.
- If you live in an apartment and suspect your neighbors of stealing your UPS packages that are left in the hall outside your apartment, create some UPS packages of your own, filling them with various containers of body fluids. The shit should stop.

NEWSPAPERS

- If you've complained to your newspaper carrier about throwing the paper in puddles of water when it rains, but to no avail, mail your next subscription payment in a Zip-loc bag full of water.

NOTARY SEALS

- To create a passable bogus notary seal, place a silver dollar tails up on a stool. Then place the document over the coin and stand on the coin/document with a clean, rubber-healed shoe. This "notarized"0 document won't stand close inspection, but how often have you ever seen any U.S. official pay that close attention to anything?

NUCLEAR INDUSTRY

- Plaster thousands of bogus radioactive warning signs along highways in states through which nuclear wastes are being transported as a protest against nuclear waste shipments.

NURSES

- When you're ordered by a drill sergeant nurse to provide a urine sample, arrive with a little container of apple juice. She'll give you a cup and point you to the little room. Follow her orders, go into the room, wait a few seconds, and exit the room carrying the paper cup now filled with apple juice. Approach the nurse who is awaiting your specimen and drink the specimen glass of apple juice.

OBITUARIES

- Send a believable obituary announcement to your local paper in your target's name. If the paper phones to check the details, your target will be shocked. If it doesn't check and the obit gets published, your target will be really shocked when she reads the torn-out page that you have anonymously mailed.

OFFICES

- If a co-worker is making you miserable, hover near her phone without being too obvious and occasionally answer it when she isn't there. Cheerfully take important messages, but don't pass them along. If someone else takes a message for her, sneak it off her desk and throw it away. She'll miss beauty appointments, business meetings, doctor appointments, and other important meetings.
- If you take a call from your obnoxious co-worker's wife when he's away from his desk, tell her that "his wife called in sick for him today."
- If your mark is trying to sell something through a classified ad and has listed the office phone number in the ad, answer all calls from prospective buyers, "Sorry, that's already been sold."
- If your co-worker mark has a WATS line, when he's not in the office, use it to call massage parlors, bars, and motels in other cities. Also, get phone numbers of some of his out-of-state relatives from his Rolodex and give them a call. Hang up as soon as they answer—the call will still be recorded on his monthly WATS statement. His boss will surely call him on his use of the business line for personal phone calls.
- If your co-worker victim has a beautiful plant on her desk, slip it a little drink of saltwater.
- If you have a real bitch boss, make her think she has a problem with vaginal odor. Get a heavy-duty magnet and an empty, unwashed can of oil-packed tuna, and attach the can to the rearmost part of her metal desk.
- Use fax machines to send very personal messages to ex-sweeties, co-workers, and others who have done you a bad deed.

OIL COMPANIES

- If you're tired of paying high gas prices to oil companies that are owned by some of the wealthiest people in the world, make them pay a little by collecting a bunch of heavy rocks and boxing them up in a sturdy carton that you mark "Caution, Geological Core Samples." Address the carton to the oil company and use its address as the return address. The company will have to pay some good-sized postal charges. Do this more than once.

- Get your hands on an internal memo from the target oil company and have your printer create some blank memo sheets using the company logo. Then, using a safe IBM typewriter and following the company's memo style, write from one oil company manager to another. The memo should discuss something sensitive such as the need to prevent leakage of financial contributions to state and national political officials for favors. Then leak the memo to the press.

- Using your target oil company's logo, have your printer make some invitations to attend a special function hosted by the oil company. The invitation should admit the bearer and a guest for entertainment and buffet on (day and date) from (time to time) and at (location). Send the invitation to a bunch of prominent citizens just a day or so before the nonevent to eliminate time for doubters and cynics to ascertain the validity of the invitation.

- If you're fed up with the major oil companies raking in untaxed windfall profits, get credit cards from as many companies as you can, using the name of a fake company and a post office box. Charge as many products and services as possible from company-owned stations, running up bills as high and as fast as possible. String them along for a couple of month, and then dissolve the company and cancel the post office box.

- If an oil company is drilling a noisy, sloppy gas well near your home, wait until it is finished drilling for the day and get some of that slimy, mucky gunk that the drillers bail out of the well. Take a couple of bucket loads of the gunk to one of the company's own gas stations and dump it on its land or, if you can, into its bulk tanks.

PAINT

- Find a wall, car, window, or whatever else your mark considers to be sacred. Spray paint nasty graffiti on it, such as satanic or Nazi art or obscenities. When the mark discovers your artwork he will pay dearly to have it cleaned up. There's the rub—you've used spray hair dye, which washes out with water.

- Ma Bell says to be careful when you paint the walls around the phone, because paint can block a proper telephone connection. Take that information and run with it.

PARANOIA

- Drop a business card belonging to a "private investigator" in your paranoid prey's yard or on his front stoop. Then get a friend to follow him in an obvious way, making notes in a book. When spotted, your accomplice should hold the target's gaze for a moment before running off. Add to the paranoia by leaving a cheap recording device near your target's vehicle or home. It should look as though it was dropped by someone who was in a hurry to get away.

- Slip a note on your mark's desk at work that says, "You are being watched." Place another one under his front door at home that says the same thing. Leave similar notes other places you know your mark will see them. Put a bumper sticker on his car bearing the same message. Finally, if you know from which vending machine your mark gets his newspapers, get to the vending machine ahead of him and stick a note bearing the cryptic message in each of the papers. By now, your mark will be checking his rearview mirror, keeping his curtains closed and jumping at the sound of his phone ringing. Who knows, if his powers of imagination are strong enough, he may even feel the need to move out of town.

- Send your mark an official-looking letter from the Center for Disease Control in Atlanta, Georgia, stating that there have been suspected incidents of people possibly contracting AIDS in his area from mosquitoes (ticks, flies). Include three "test strips" with the letter that you have made by soaking blotter paper in a strong cobalt chloride solution and drying thoroughly (these will immediately turn blue when exposed to moisture). They should be stamped with control numbers or lot numbers for authenticity. The letter then instructs the target to urinate on a test strip, indicating that a change from white or light pink to a strong blue or purple is a positive indicator of AIDS— and in that case, he should immediately have any/all sexual partners take the same test using the remaining test strips. Instruct him to report to the local VD clinic if results are positive.

PARKING LOTS

- If your car's been damaged in one of those parking lots featuring spikes that blow out the tires of cars going the wrong way, and the owner refuses to pay you for your damage, remove the steel cover plate over the spikes and, using a ratchet wrench, loosen the spikes' connecting rod. Then turn

the rod the other way so the spikes are facing departing traffic. The cheapskate manager will have more angry customers than just you to deal with.

PARKING TICKETS

- If your mark gets a lot of parking tickets, remove several tickets from her car at various times before she sees them. Then, using one of those novelty rubber stamps that features an upraised middle finger, stamp a message on the tickets and return the mark's tickets to the police. If you don't have such a stamp, print or type some foul message insulting to police on the tickets, draw something on it, or blow your nose on it. Don't include any money, of course.

PARTY TIME

- Send out 200 invitations to a barbecue party at your victim's home asking guests to bring their own bottle to make things appear legitimate. Even if the victim gets wind of the trick, he'll never know who all was invited, and so he won't be able to stop them all from coming.
- If your mark is having a party and you know the time, call the police and complain that the party is too loud or phone all his neighbors and invite them all to the party.
- Visit a few seedy, smelly, old-fart bars on a Saturday night and have a few friendly beers with as many of the patrons as you can. Posing as your mark, invite them all to a party at his house early Sunday afternoon. It should be time for them to be ready for a little hair of the dog.
- Put posters up in the low-income areas of

town announcing free lunch with one of your local not-so-upstanding politicians. Use words like "all you can eat" and "beer, wine, or soda included with your meal." Don't forget to mention a time and place. Hundreds of hungry, thirsty, and highly irritated people will remember who *not* to vote for in the next election.

- Have an accomplice arrive at a party thrown by your mark and, when the time is right, add a plate of candied laxatives to the munchie table.
- If you know your mark is having a party on any given day or night, arrange to have the utilities shut off at that time.

PEEPING TOMS

- To give a peeping Tom a bigger shock than he'd hoped for, booby-trap the window frame by hooking one pole of a capacitor to an aluminum-frame window and grounding the other, putting DMSO and croton oil (defecating agent) or DMSO and syrup of ipecac (vomiting agent) on the window ledge, putting commercial itching powder or poison-oak extract/leaves on the window ledge, rigging a photo flash to take a picture of the peeper and temporarily blind him at the same time, putting razor blades or broken glass on the window ledge, or leaving marking dye on the window ledge.
- Plant roses, blackberries, cactus, or poison oak outside the window.
- Rig water sprays that can be turned on from the inside near the window.
- Leave broken glass or roofing nails on the ground outside the window.
- Unleash your hostile dog on the intruder.
- Aim a good, strong laser at any telescopes you see targeted on your windows.

PEN PALS

- Invent a horny, seductive lady who wants your mark to become her pen pal. Using a post office box as your return address, through a series of increasingly personal letters, build a desire in the mark by teasing with all sorts of props like flowers, hints of gifts, bogus sexy photos, and the like. Just before the final step, discontinue the postal box. The last thing you do is mail, call, or telegram a final message, "Meet you at the Sin City Hotel, suite 625, tonight at 10 P.M. I'll have the tub and me all warm and wet."

PERSONAL

- It's easy to turn your mark into a fabled thief by getting a full-face photo of him, plus a furtive longer shot of the type usually taken by surveillance cameras. Take these pictures and your warning copy to a trusted printer and get some posters made. Display his name and picture along with big headlines about him being a thief, shoplifter, or pickpocket. Make it sound realistic and sign it by the local community's merchants association and then take the posters to neighborhood stores and hang them up without being seen. You can use the same procedure identifying your mark as a sex offender, child molester, or pornographer.
- Write horrible news stories about your mark and have your printer set them in newspaper style, complete with columns and a dateline naming a town in which your mark formerly lived. The bogus news stories could be about the mark's child molestation, sexual perversion, child abuse, kitten killing, puppy beating, fawn poaching, public

flashing, and so on. Make the story sound authentic and then send copies to the mark's employer, family, and friends. Have the mail postmarked from the dateline city and include a short note saying you think people ought to know the truth.

- Get some 3-methyl-11-butane-thiol at a chemical supply store and, when your mark is all dressed up for an important appointment and being jostled around by a crowd, squirt some of it on her. It smells like skunk.
- Dip your fingers into some warm water, come up behind your mark, and as you deliver an ear-shattering sneeze, fling the water on the mark's neck or back. This works well with backless dresses or at the pool.
- If you have no doubt that your soon-to-be-ex-feller has been sleeping around, wait till he's asleep one night and gently apply some superglue to his penis and his leg.

PERVERSIONS

- If the victim coaches a Little League team or is involved with kids in any way, anonymously inform the father (preferably a rough redneck) of one of the boys that the victim has been making advances toward the boy.
- If the mark takes regular walks, call one of his neighbors and angrily report that he's flashing children. Tell them you're a passing motorist who witnessed his disgusting, perverted act.
- Tack up notices around the neighborhood saying your mark is a homosexual, cross-dresser, or child molester. Give specific dates and times when he supposedly committed these offenses.

PETS

- If your mark's dog or cat doesn't wear a collar, call the city pound and ask officials to pick up the "stray" that is acting rabid and threatening your children.
- Send the victim's children an ant farm with a note saying the gift is from an out-of-town uncle. Bore a tiny hole in an inconspicuous place so that the ants can escape inside the victim's home.
- If your neighbor's pets are annoying, put a scare into your neighbor by tossing bite-sized balls of raw hamburger over the fence along with an empty box of rat poison. The animal will be fine, but your target will likely put out a few bucks on veterinary bills.
- If your target raises show dogs, mist the pooches with a strong solution of food coloring just before a show.
- If your target has longhaired animals, clip them or clip a brief (but appropriate) message into their fur.
- If your mark's dog is scheduled to be in a show, go to the show, dog whistle in hand, and when your mark's dog is in the ring, just give a little whistle.
- If your mark breeds purebreds for show or sale, wait till the little bitches are in heat and introduce them to a horny old mutt.
- If your mark keeps her dog locked up indoors with little or no exercise, feed the animal some hard-boiled eggs. The next day your mark should be looking for a bit of fresh air. Who knows, maybe she'll even take the dog.
- Add gelatin to your mark's goldfish bowl. It will turn the residents into a lovely fish-in-aspic.
- If your mark has ornamental fish—koi (read: expensive), for example—have an

accomplice fillet and pan-fry it and serve it to your mark. You can either enjoy the revenge quietly or leave a box in a prominent place containing the inedible but identifiable remains.

- Grab a couple of your mark's goldfish. When they've stopped gasping for air, lay them to rest between two slices of bread. Add a little lettuce and mayo and serve it all up with a couple of Pringles—goldfish and chips to go.

PHOTOGRAPHY

- If you're competent in photography, darkroom techniques, and minor retouching/airbrushing, composite photographs could be useful to you. Your photos can show your mark leaving a motel room with a person of the opposite sex, or your mark's spouse nude and in a compromising pose with an animal companion or a person of the same sex.
- If you get teed off about having to deal with a rude department store clerk, take a photo of her ignoring other customers while she's casually filing her fingernails and mail the photo to her manager. She'll likely find herself with time for a pedicure too.
- If your target is a right-wing photography buff, it might be fun to put him in a compromising situation. Buy a roll of the film he normally uses, carefully remove it from the box and use it to take pictures of pictures in the sickest hard-core magazines you can lay your hands on. Flatten the magazine and prevent glare with a piece of nonreflective glass, and take the pictures in close so as to obscure the page numbers and edges of the photos. Now rewind the film carefully, leaving the end tag poking

out like in a new roll. Put it back in the box and reglue the open end. Your target will use it sooner or later and, even later, will have a fine set of double exposures for his (and the photo shop's or the vice squad's) viewing pleasure.

PHOTO SHOPS

- If your local photo shop doesn't like your lively pictures and do-it-yourself porn, and refuses to develop your film, run ads on behalf of the lab either in the local establishment media or in the underground press. The ads should claim things like, "We develop anything . . . no questions asked . . . We love dirty pix too . . . We buy your good stuff—the raunchier, the better." Sign the ads with the name of the lab or its owner.

PITCH

- Soft pitch (resin) found in little blisters of the newer bark of most any balsam-family tree is free and handy. Collect it on a knife blade and apply it to doorknobs, toilet seats, tool handles, and so on.

POLICE

- When you see your mark drive away from home or his office, call the police and report your car stolen. Describe his auto and report the direction he's heading.
- If you know your mark's been drinking and you see him drive away, report him to the police as a drunk driver. Say that he almost ran you off the road.
- If your victim is a door-to-door salesman,

follow him to the neighborhood where he's working that day. Then call the police and say you're a resident of that neighborhood and complain that the mark's bothering or threatening you. Describe him and his car to the police

- Late at night, after your victim and his family have gone to bed, call the police and report that you saw a man sneaking around his home and give a general physical description that matches the victim.
- Call the police and report that you heard gunshots and screams coming from your mark's home.

POLITICS

- If you have $25 and 25 signatures, you can run for public office. This gives you a legal platform to attack and ridicule the institutions and people who deserve such attention.
- If your mark/political VIP is planning a photo shoot for the local newspaper with the local Asian community, hire some of the citizens of that neighborhood to appear in the background of the photo holding a large banner spelling out a slogan in their native characters. The slogan should mention some questionable behavior by the mark, such as receiving under-the-table campaign donations.
- Have some fortune cookies made that contain messages questioning your mark/political VIP's integrity. Pass them out at your VIP's political rally.
- Pay someone to streak naked outside your political mark's hotel room shouting, "I love (mark's name)."
- If your mark is a not-so-well-known weasel-like political candidate, hire an actor who is

a real look-alike for the politician and have the ringer travel the state for a week giving controversial and asinine speeches and press conferences in the real politician's name.

POLLS

- Get the names of survey organizations and let them know your mark is interested in participating in every poll they take. He'll be harassed beyond belief with phone calls and forms to fill out.

POOP

- Order a turd sent to your victim through the mail.
- The next time your neighbor's cat or dog dumps a load in your yard or garden, have a pretty gift box stuffed with tissue paper handy. Add the crap and another layer of tissue, wrap it up pretty, and mail it to your mark.

PORNOGRAPHY

- Send the victim's name and address to one of the multitude of companies that sell pornographic items by mail. His name will be placed on a national mailing list, and he will be bombarded with porno brochures. The government might also add his name to its list of order-by-mail perverts and harass him accordingly.
- Mail batches of soft-core porno pictures to your victim's home and office with a note saying, "Here are the photos you ordered."
- If your mark is someone who would censor literature or otherwise impose her own

personal beliefs upon you under penalty of law, prepare some address labels using her name and address, and place them on some really sleazy magazines featuring kiddie porn and sex with animals. Leave a few magazines in doctors' or dentists' waiting rooms, Sunday school reading rooms, and the periodical shelves of your local library.

POSTAL SERVICE

- Place your stamps in the lower right corners of envelopes. The automatic canceling machine will miss them, and someone can reuse the stamps.
- File change-of-address cards for your mark's home and business addresses.
- If you have two targets and they happen to be enemies too, file change-of-address cards for both of them, having mail from one target directed to the other and vice versa.
- To get back at a post office that has misplaced a check or important letter, jam its system with dead letters. This is done by sending loads of letters containing blank paper to nonexistent addresses with no return address. Use one-cent stamps or, better yet, used stamps. When the letters cannot be delivered and there is no return address, they will go to the dead-letter office.

POSTERS

- Collect posters of your favorite politician target and affix them to the walls behind the urinals in men's rest rooms. A little target practice never hurt anyone.
- If you have an incumbent president you don't like, make up some posters saying "(Name of president): WANTED FOR TREASON," and hang them all over town. Your kicker is that you put your mark's name in small type as the sponsor of the poster, then list some affiliation such as the Klan, the Birchers, the Nazis, or the U.S. Labor Party under his name.

PRINTING

- Print up some official-looking envelopes with a return address such as the county health department and the words HERPES TEST RESULTS or AIDS TEST RESULTS printed in large letters. Put several sheets of paper in the envelope to give it bulk and print the words PERSONAL AND CONFIDENTIAL on the envelope. This works especially well when you know that your mark will be going out of town on vacation and his neighbor will be collecting his mail for him.
- Other examples of effective words to put on official-looking envelopes are PROBATION OFFICER, PRISONER WORK RELEASE PROGRAM, CHILD ABUSE CENTER, WIFE-BEATERS ANONYMOUS, and KLEPTOMANIAC CENTER.
- Print up a phony draft notice and send it to your mark. He might be stupid enough to go down and enlist.
- Phony quarantine posters work well when tailored to the target. The day before a horse show, hit 'em with one for equestrian anthrax; before a cattle auction, one for hoof-and-mouth disease; before a bird show, one for parrot fever; and so on.
- Put up a notice of property tax sale a day or two before your target plans to go on vacation. Or post it while he's away, along with a notice of who bought it at

the auction. Use another target's name as the purchaser.

- Deliver phony notices to appear for jury duty or notices of bench warrants issued. The best is a notice that your mark is being sued for divorce, outlining how badly he is about to get fleeced.
- Have an accomplice deliver a phony "palimony" suit to your target, making sure his wife is there to receive delivery.

PROJECTILES

- A thin-shelled paint grenade can be made using the basics of that old childhood game of pinholing the two ends of an egg and then blowing out the gloop. Use a needle and syringe to fill the empty shell with colorful, permanent drawing ink. Close with glue, locate your mark, and toss.

PUBLIC UTILITIES

- Call the telephone, water, and power companies, using the victim's name, and say you would like your service discontinued because you are moving out of town. Supply a "forwarding address" and ask that your final bill be sent there. Do this on a Friday and your victim won't get

services resumed until at least Monday.

- Call the telephone company and have your mark's phone number changed to an unlisted number. It will bill him for this service, and when he calls to find out his new number, it won't let him have it.
- Shoot holes into transformers to destroy an electric utility's property.
- Shoot the insulators on the high-tension lines.
- Smash power meters on vacation homes to keep your target electric company busy. Do it after the routine meter reading and just before a long holiday weekend. Do it to several meters in a large area. The owners of the vacation homes will be sure to shed their ire upon the offending electric company.
- Request service from utility companies to vacant houses or lots.
- Tamper with your enemy's meter and report it to the utility company.

PUZZLES

- Do crossword and other puzzle freaks bother you, always asking you to help them solve their damn puzzles? Next time, pretend to study all the cross clues and then fill in a bunch of close-but-wrong answers in ink. Apologize to the puzzler for your mistake. He probably won't ask for your help in the future.

RADAR

- Radio frequency interference indicators (RFI) blank out a radar gun's speed display window whenever there is any type of electromagnetic voltage interference. You can key the mike on your mobile CB in the proximity of a radar gun, and it will kick on the RFI and render the gun useless. The limit on distance is about one-quarter of a mile.

RADIO STATIONS

- If your target is a radio station that broadcasts live from your favorite sporting event, secure a seat as close as possible to the broadcasting booth and take along your ghetto blaster, having disconnected the speakers first. Tune the radio in to your target station and turn the volume to high and the tone knob to maximum treble. This will cause massive feedback that your target won't be able to do anything about.
- Call about 50 people from the telephone directory and, after making them identify themselves, read out a written statement, something like, "Congratulations (person's name), you have won the (name of radio station mark) free telephone sweepstakes. This is not a gimmick or a sale. Our computer has selected just five names at random from the phone book, and yours is

one of them. To collect your $5,000 cash prize, call (target radio station's phone number) and ask for (target DJ's name)."

RAILROADS

- Set the manual brakes on railroad cars. This will cause a great deal of time delay for checking and rechecking, tying up people, time, and money.
- Visit the rail yard areas on cold, cold nights and pour lots of water on the switch points. This freezes the switches, making them inoperable.

RAPE

- An Arizona inventor named Charles Barlow has come up with a nifty little antirape device, which now carries a U.S. Patent Office registration number. In effect, he has developed a vagina harpoon. The vaginal harpoon is a tiny base housing a tinier yet compressible coil spring covered with a soft plastic cloth. A thin reed of surgical steel with a pointed, harpoon-like tip is embedded in the center of the coil. The device is inserted into the vagina with the aid of a tube and a lubricant, much the same as a tampon. When the vagina is visited by an unwanted male protrusion, the coil is compressed and the harpoon is activated, solidly impaling the intruder's member on his first (and, by the way, last) thrust. The inventor claims that when the horribly pained male quickly withdraws, he pulls the contraption out with him because of the barbed tip of the harpoon. He also claims that professional medical assistance will be required to remove the device safely, which will enable a doctor to identify a rapist to the appropriate authorities.

- Spray lye-based oven cleaner in the face of a would-be rapist. It makes for easy identification. Just tell the police it was the blind guy with blisters.

RATS

- Buy and breed some big, dirty, mean Norwegian rats. They're cheap to keep, multiply quickly, and make people really unhappy.
- Rats and mice can cause quite a stir in restaurants and other establishments where hygiene is paramount. If you've been dealt some dirt by one of these businesses, on a busy night, carry a rat or a couple of mice into the place in a box. Set it under your table while you eat and just before you leave, kick the lid off the box and get theatrical about the huge rat you've just seen crawling across the floor.
- If you can't find a live rodent, a dead one will suffice. Dump it in the restaurant as you are leaving so some other patron will find it, or, put the body in a glass jar, add two inches of water, and screw the lid on tightly. Put the jar somewhere it won't be found for a couple of days like behind a planter. The decaying rat will eventually release enough noxious gas and build up enough pressure to explode the jar. Just deserts for a smelly rat of the two-legged variety.

RECORD DEPARTMENTS

- If you have been hassled or cheated by a record store that sells low-quality goods, buy or borrow a small portable eraser from your local electronics store. Whichever you use, wave it fast over the tape display repeatedly. It works.

RECORDS AND BOOKS

- Use various mail drops and order lots of introductory offers from mail-order book and record clubs. After the initial deliveries, send the bills back with the word "Deceased" written on them, and cancel post office boxes and other mail drops you used in the process.
- Put your target's collection of old record albums in the oven and bake at 350 degrees for 30 minutes or until dissolved.

REDECORATING

- If you know your mark is ordering new furniture, draperies, carpeting, or the like, call the company later and cancel the order, or order different colors or styles.

RELATIONSHIPS

- If the victim's wife is pregnant, phone him and say, "The child your wife is carrying isn't yours," and quickly hang up.
- If your husband has been stepping out on

you, find out where he meets his newfound friend and enlist the help of a girlfriend that your husband doesn't know. She should either have a young baby of her own or have a baby niece or nephew for whom she could "baby-sit" for a couple of hours. Have your friend walk into the bar carrying the baby, approach your husband, and say, "So this is where you've been spending your evenings while I'm home taking care of little Charlene. You rat!" Your husband will be baffled, but his claims not to know who your friend and the baby are will fall on deaf ears.

- If you've been living with a partner for some time and find out he's on the make, before you give him that fond farewell, make sure you copy down the numbers and expiration dates of his credit cards. Then when he's gone, soothe your broken heart by making phone orders using his cards. You could even order some neat stuff for him . . . turds by mail, gay magazine subscriptions, saltpeter.
- Posing as your target's phantom lover, write a "Dear John/Jane" letter, saying something along the lines of, "It was fun while it lasted—no regrets—but I can't stand the thought of breaking up a happy marriage. Please, forget about getting a divorce." Fold it up to make it look like it's been mailed, received, and read, and slip it into your target's pocket, car, purse, or wherever his or her spouse might conceivably find it.
- Phone your blissfully in-love ex at the office and leave a message saying her new partner has been involved in an accident and is seriously injured. Give the name of a hospital a long way away.
- Apply superglue to the locks of your soon-to-be-ex-partner's baggage before he leaves, but after he packs to leave you.
- Smear one side of your soon-to-be-ex-

partner's suitcase with superglue and stick it to the television screen or glue up the TV remote control.

- Superglue your ex-partner's favorite CDs inside their cases.
- Remind your ex-partner that you promised you'd always stick together by gluing book and photo album pages together, canned food to the cupboard shelves, cups and saucers to one another or to the table. Glue the telephone handset to the cradle, glue the lids on the liquor bottles, glue down the toilet seat lid . . .

RELIGION

- Call or visit one of the local whacko religious sects and ask a representative to come meditate with you (aka your mark) and your family.
- Collect a bunch of cards from those church pushers who flock to your front porch and the next time one shows up, hand her a card and say, "I'm not interested, but here's someone who is."
- When those persistent religious salespeople appear on your doorstep, act like you're interested in what they have to say and then start asking kinky personal questions.
- When religious zealots refuse to leave after you've asked them to politely, listen to what they have to say and look normal but persistently scratch your genitals. When you notice them looking, apologize and tell them it's just your crabs.
- When you see the suited boys on the bikes riding up your driveway, get ready for them. Come to the door stark naked. If that doesn't faze them, invite them in to discuss your beliefs—reincarnation and the laying on of hands.

RESTAURANTS

- If you're tired of a local eatery charging you for terrible food or a bad atmosphere, add a little silver nitrate to the liquid soap dispenser in the rest room. It will leave customers' and employees' hands and faces unwashably stained to an ugly, erratic brown color.

- If you know your mark will be dining in a posh restaurant in the company of friends, you go, too, and take an elegantly printed card with you that reads, "The management requests that you and your party leave immediately before we have to call the authorities." Tip a waiter to deliver it to the mark.

- Smuggle a dead cockroach into a swanky eatery and order the best thing on the menu. About halfway through the meal, hide your late friend under the garnish on your plate and turn on the theatrics. Fuss about your health, the restaurant's cleanliness standards, and use the phrase "my lawyer" every so often. Allow the management to talk you into a free meal or two and some drinks.

- Run a small display ad for your target restaurant in a campus newspaper or small local newspaper or shopper that isn't professional enough to do much checking. Offer some fantastic dinner bargain like two-for-one steak dinners or all-you-can-eat crab legs when the clipped ad is presented between 6 and 7 that night. By 8 P.M., the owner could have a lot of ex-customers and a bad reputation that will be hard to overcome. To save face, he might decide to honor the ad, to the tune of more than a couple of bucks.

- If you're repeatedly ignored by a waitress, drop her tip—a couple of pennies—into a glass of water, put a piece of paper across the top of the glass, and turn it upside down on the table. That ought to get her attention.

- If your target restaurant has a help-yourself salad bar, a dead mouse could appear in the cottage cheese, live maggots could be set among the cold chicken wings, and a fat slug would look authentic squirming around in the bowl of lettuce.

- Squirt a dollop of mayo into a condom and stick it under some macaroni salad at your local serve-yourself-some salad place.

- If your target eatery is one of those all-you-can eat buffets, go to the nearest skid row and collect about a dozen hungry and odoriferous homeless people and offer to get them a meal. Take them to your targeted buffet, settle them down, and order a meal for each of them. Now sit back and enjoy while your hungry yet aromatic new friends empty the salad bar and the restaurant simultaneously. The manager could kick them all out, but how would it look to throw out a bunch of starving people, especially if some generous soul has offered to pay for them?

- Give your target restaurant a hand with its menu. You can type up a menu just like the restaurant's own, listing all their specialties, but at exorbitant prices or at prices so low it'll go broke. Or you could list offensive dishes like Puppy Sausages, Baked Rat Entrails, or Sheep's Eye Rockefeller. Now visit the restaurant and remove its loose menus from the covers and substitute your own or, if you can find a way to gain access to the glass menu display box many restaurants have outside, slip your new and improved menu in it in place of the real thing.

- Paste a sign over the display box menu of your target eatery saying, "Closed for private party."

- Send an advertisement in your mark restaurant's name to your local newspaper announcing that you will be closed a month for remodeling.
- Send official-looking Department of Health letters to people living in the vicinity of your target restaurant saying that several people have developed infectious hepatitis after eating at your target restaurant. Urge them to go to their infectious disease clinic for a checkup if they have eaten at the restaurant in the last two months.
- Plant animal parts in your mark restaurant's trash. Fresh roadkill is easy to find. Then anonymously notify the health inspectors that you suspect the restaurant is substituting dog and cat meat.

RETURN ENVELOPES

- Always salvage business reply envelopes you receive in the mail from institutions, businesses, government agencies, and so on. Especially good are envelopes that were not sealed well or that you opened without tearing. They make great containers for sending materials to your mark, as they identify a second mark for the first mark to puzzle over as she ponders "why me" in reference to the contents of your parcel.

ROADKILL

- Watch for small dead animals (dogs, cats, mice, birds) in the road. Pick them up, wrap them in airtight containers, wait a week, and then have them delivered to the victim's home.

- Put a collar on a fresh dog or cat corpse and tie a sturdy string to it. Secure the other end of the string around your mark's bumper and hide the animal under the car so your mark won't see it before driving away. The police and the SPCA think this blatant cruelty to animals is a real drag.
- Tie a sturdy piece of string around the neck of a fresh animal corpse and set it on a skateboard. Position it on one side of the road along the route your target usually takes home from work. Holding the other end of the string, hide yourself on the other side of the road until you see your target driving close. As he does, pull hard on the string to drag the animal across the road in front of your mark. If he's such a jerk he doesn't even stop to see the carnage he's just caused, at least he'll have to clean some nasty stuff off his car.
- Drop a supply of ripe roadkill where your target's favorite dog can get to it. The dog will think he died and went to heaven while he rolls around in the stuff, and then later, he'll want to jump up on his master to thank him.
- If your roadkill is ripe enough for its skin to slip off, remove the skin and put a disposable diaper on the leftovers. Place the mess in a plastic bag with some baby clothes, dump it in the target's garbage, and dial 911.

ROCK STARS

- Advertise that a cult rock or film star will make a nonscheduled appearance at your mark's store. You have no idea what sort of damage will be caused by a few hundred hard-core fans when their idol doesn't show up and the ugly word "hoax" goes through the crowds. You should be there to spread the word.

ROOFS

- If you've been screwed by a roofing company that not only overcharged you but did a tacky job to boot, toss a couple of bars of plain bath soap into the tar baths used by the roofing company. It makes the tar bubble over in all the wrong places, and it will take some time to clean up the mess and cost money to settle potential lawsuits for the spillage.

ROOMMATES

- If you share a house and are tired of your tight-ass roommates helping themselves to your goodies, teach them a lesson. Buy a syringe and use it to inject liquid detergent into whatever it is your thieving housemates like to eat. They'll be spending more time in the bathroom and less in the kitchen.

RUBBERS

- Drop a used rubber on the rear floorboard of the victim's car.
- If you have easy access to your mark's rubbers (no, not that kind, the kind he wears on his shoes) on a winter or rainy day, and you know when he is going to be putting them on, pour some slow-drying glue into the footwear a bit before they go over his shoes.

SALES REPRESENTATIVES

- If your mark works in a store or any other place that deals directly with the public, get your pals to call the manager and complain about the shoddy treatment she has been giving them. Say she's rude, ignored them, or showed no interest in doing the job she's paid to do. After enough complaints, your mark will have to look for another job, and when she finds one, give your friends that phone number and have them do an encore.

SALESPEOPLE

- Next time you receive one of those letters from a time-share company informing you that you've definitely won a prize and all you have to do is come and listen to an hour-long sales spiel about the joys of time share, take 'em up in it, but take up a little of the high-pressure salesperson's time in exchange for your own. Act interested, tell him you want to buy three weeks, haggle a little, ask for a discount, hem and haw about the locations you want, and ask a lot of tedious questions. Get them to phone you at home and go on about how you need to talk to your bank. In the end, when you've agreed to everything, the papers are all drawn up, and you're ready to sign, say, "Oh, I was only kidding," and walk away.

SCHOOLS

- Draw or paste something obscene on pull-down maps and screens.
- Institute massive searches for "lost" contact lenses during particularly dull assemblies or lessons.
- Varnish the blackboards using a can of artist's spray varnish.
- If your school uses white boards and magic markers, spray varnish on the boards after you've used the magic markers to leave an appropriate message.
- Free captured animals and insects being held prisoner for use in biology experiments.
- Get some school letterhead and put up some "official" notices around the school regarding new rules.

SECRETS

- If you're aware of something your victim wants to keep secret (he cheated a friend on a business deal, cheated on his wife, cheated on his income tax), write or call the people involved and tell them about it.

SECURITY

- Sometimes you just want to keep some aspect of your mark secure. Locks, chains, and cables are great for closing lanes and driveways, sealing vehicles in or out, keeping people in offices, homes, apartments, or even buildings. They can fasten objects (read "bumpers") to other objects.

SEWAGE

- If you have a big old camper with, say, a 25-gallon holding tank for the mobile sewer system, and you know your mark will be away on vacation for a week or so, take several loads of the stuff over to his place and spray it all over his lawn, shrubs, and patio.

SEX

- Having trouble with an obscene caller? Arrange to meet him in a bar in a couple of hours. Just don't tell him you intend to also invite the police.
- Console yourself after the painful ending of a love affair by going through the old photo albums and picking out shots you took of her in bed. Get a few (50) prints made or make 50 copies of the photo on a color Xerox and slip them under the windshield wipers at her office parking lot.
- Want to hit an ex-boyfriend where it really hurts? Send him a get-well-soon card and a tube of penis-enlarger cream (check the ads in smutty magazines).
- If your target is one who regularly entertains a friend at a quiet hotel, get access to a computer, dummy up your very

own Hideaway Hotel Frequent Customer Club cards, and invite your target to join. Send the invitation to home or work—whichever address will likely offer an audience for the opening.
- Advertise phone sex in your mark's name. Make your invitation as hot and horny as you can and provide your target's mobile phone as the bell to ring.
- If your target is a homophobe, enlist an ambitious drag queen to help you out. Wait until your target and his wife are at a fancy restaurant and have your accomplice (dressed to kill) confront their table, point at his wife, and in a very loud, very offended voice scream, "Who's the bitch?" Then, "I knew you were still in the closet, but I didn't know you were using a cover"; "I wondered where you got those crabs from; I can't believe you could put me at risk this way"; and "It's her or me. Ditch the bitch or it's over!" Then your thespian friend should beat a hasty retreat.
- If your target is a homophobe, when he's at a party with a lady friend, get a pretty male friend to shout, "Stop looking at my dick, you creep!"
- If your target is an insecure macho male, you could forge a shy, nervous letter from him to his male boss or a friend declaring his passionate love. Explain that this feeling has been growing for some time and that "I just don't want to live a lie anymore."
- If you want to target a two-timing woman, take her out to an expensive restaurant and order the most extravagant things on the menu. Just after the first course arrives, leap to your feet and shout, "Pregnant? You never did that with me!" Then storm out of the place, leaving her to face the bill and the spectators.
- Fill a couple of inflatable sex dolls with

helium and put them in your target's trunk. He'll be surprised when he opens the trunk and the babes float out, but not as surprised as he will be when they are returned by finders demanding payment. You, of course, would have fixed each of the floating foxes with a note saying, "I belong to (target's name and office address). If your find me please return me." Offer a generous reward for their return.

SKATEBOARDERS

- If you have a problem with skateboarders rudely mowing pedestrians down on the pavement, scatter a handful of large-caliber rifle ammunition primers in their path. You'll get a bang out of it.

SLEEPY TIME

- Chloral hydrate (knockout drops) is still available, though harder to get than in the past. Mix one gram with several dissolved saccharin tablets to camouflage the bitter taste before serving it to your mark. Seconal mixed with the mark's beer will also serve to put him to sleep in about 15 minutes. Be warned, however, seconal is a powerful downer and can be deadly.

SLINGSHOTS

- Giant slingshots that are five feet tall and need to be anchored into the ground can be used to propel large fruits and vegetables against the home of the neighborhood bad guy from up to 75 yards away.

SMOKERS

- If you're tired of breathing the smoke of cigarettes left to smolder in ashtrays, buy a package of sparklers and scrape the explosive coating off the wire stems, or cut them into short lengths with wire cutters. Now put some of this material into your mark's ashtrays. The next time someone leaves a burning cigarette in the ashtray or puts a cigarette out, the sparks will really fly.
- Using a long, fine needle, thread a few horse or human hairs through several of your mark's cigarettes or cigars. Trim the ends of the hairs and put the cigarettes/ cigars back into their packs. It'll give those smoking marks a whiff of their own medicine.

SNOWMEN

- If your kids have a problem with one of those lowlifes who live to ruin a tyke's good time by, for example, tearing down or driving over their freshly built snowmen, have your kids build their snowpeople around a fire hydrant, a cement pole, a tree stump, or something else that will give a person or a car equal or worse impact damage.

SNOWMOBILES

- If snowmobilers are trespassing across your property, spread monofilament line trails for them to pass over. The line gets sucked into the machine's mechanism and puts a rapid stop to this desecration of your land.

SOCIAL OCCASIONS

- If your neighbors are the kind who like to hold regular all-night bashes with the stereo turned up full-blast and nary a thought to their neighbors who just might be trying to get a little shut-eye, give them a taste of their own medicine. Next time one of the parties starts, get out your tape player and a microphone and record a good 90 minutes of the hell-raising. Next morning, nice and early—say around 6:30 or 7:00—pack yourself a picnic and head off for a quiet day, but before you go, position your tape player against the wall of your neighbor's bedroom if you live in an apartment or as close as possible if you're in a house next door. Now load the machine with the tape you recorded the previous evening, turn the volume up full-blast, and leave. If you have an auto-reverse player, your tape will just keep playing and playing . . .

- Stuff olive cavities with pieces of hot chili pepper or, if you're a fishing fan, little pieces of bait and trade them for the ones on the bar at your mark's cocktail party.

- Superglue all the bottles of booze to the bar top at your mark's next party.

- If your mark is having a snooty dinner party, secret a small pebble to the affair in your pocket. When the main course arrives, start eating, stop suddenly, choke a little, and bring your napkin up to your mouth. Having already transferred the pebble to your hand, look as if you're fishing around for something in your mouth and then pull out the pebble. Look shocked, pretend to make light of the situation while your host suffers the embarrassment.

- Call the police to quiet down your mark's party, giving the name and address of a neighbor. This is particularly fun if you're a guest at the party, because you not only have an alibi, you get to watch all the excitement.

- If your mark is a woman, wait until her birthday and she is either at a small family gathering or a romantic dinner for two. Then have flowers delivered to her with a note that says, "Flowers for my precious petal."

- Send a strip-o-gram to your mark's posh birthday celebration—the cruder the better.

- Ever gone camping to partake of the solitude, only to be blown out of the serenity by some rude campers who were obnoxious, loud, and left litter wherever they went? Send them some uninvited guests in the form of bugs by smearing cooking fat around their campsite to attract flies or crushing a package of cookies and scattering the crumbs to bring in the ants. Mix up a syrup of sugar and lemon juice and pour it into an empty insect repellent bottle; offer to lend it to the rude ones.

- If your target is fond of hosting garden parties or is planning a garden wedding reception (and you can afford it), hire a plane to fly back and forth over the party towing an embarrassing message on a banner.

STICKERS

- You can have slogans printed on permastick stickers and carry them with you to use at appropriate times. Stickers can say things like "This Machine Steals Money," "Horrible Food," "Lousy Service," "This Movie Rated Blah," "My Taxes Paid for This?" "Filthy Rest Rooms," "Inept Nerd," "Way to Park, Ace," "Rip Off," and "Rude Driver," to name just a few. Be creative.

STINK

- A small amount of butyric acid will stink up an area badly. Leave a small bottle where it can be knocked over in your enemy's house or place of business. A couple of good places to leave a little are courtrooms (to let the judge know you think his decision stinks) and movie theaters after a particularly bad film.
- Spread a little warm Limburger cheese on your target's shoes (he'll think he's got jungle rot) or in his radiators or exhaust manifold. The smell's like a Tootsie Roll . . . it lasts a long time.
- Slip a little fish sauce here and there inside your target's car or office just before an important date or meeting. Only the neighborhood alley cats will stick around.

STUDENTS

- If you were a poor kid who used to get teased a lot by other students for the hand-me-downs you wore and have since done quite well for yourself, arrive at your class reunion in a chauffeur-driven limousine.
- If a dormmate has a bad habit of coming in blotto in the middle of the night and waking everyone else up in the mean time, next time he leaves for one of his binges, use drywall to cover his dorm door, spackle over the drywall, and then paint it to match the wall color. When the drunk comes in much later, he'll spend hours crawling up and down the hall babbling about not being able to find his room.

SUBSCRIPTIONS

- Call the circulation department of your local newspaper or cable company and cancel the victim's subscription. If he doesn't subscribe to either the newspaper or cable service, sign him up.

SUBSTITUTIONS

- Substitute hair remover for hair conditioner on the ledge in your mark's shower.
- Vinegar can be substituted for nose drops or, if you're really evil, eyedrops, but before choosing to take someone's sight away remember the old adage an eye for an eye . . . karma, mind you.

SUPERGLUE

- Superglue the door locks on a police car when the police are shaking someone down or enjoying a coffee and donut break.
- Superglue the boss' briefcase shut just before an important meeting.
- Superglue the switches that turn on networked computers in large offices.
- A drop of superglue on a floppy disk will stop your mark's program.
- Superglue the lock on your nerd/mark's floppy disk file box. He won't be able to function without the disks.
- Put a drop of superglue in the ignition lock of your neighbor's loud motorcycle.
- Put a drop of superglue in your enemy's post office box lock.
- Superglue the locks on the coin boxes of pay phones.
- Superglue the locks of display cases at jewelry stores.

- Superglue the locks on the courtroom doors during the noon recess.
- Superglue your mark's telephone to its base.
- Superglue the threads of a burned-out light bulb and return it to its socket in your mark's desk lamp.
- Superglue a single paper clip to your mark's desk.
- Superglue glasses, dishes, and silverware to the tables in a bad restaurant just before rush hour.
- Superglue cans and jars to the shelves in supermarkets.
- Superglue the pages of often-used reference books in the county clerk's office.
- Superglue the microfiche together at the county assessor's office.
- If your target fancies himself a real Romeo, superglue his dimmer switches in the full bright position.

SUPERMARKETS

- Remove the policy notice from the bulletin board of a supermarket chain store that you feel has in some way ripped you off. Cut off the letterhead and create new blank sheets of letterhead with the aid of a photocopy machine. Call the corporation and get a couple of the vice-presidents' names. Then using a rental electric typewriter, type a very nice letter to several of your least favorite acquaintances, telling them they have won a TV set or $200 worth of free groceries and that they should come to their local store on Saturday (when corporate headquarters will be closed) to claim their prize. Sign a VP's name on the letter.
- Inject store-brand milk containers with a little lemon juice.
- Load a grocery cart with frozen foods and ice cream and abandon it on a busy day when it won't be noticed for hours.
- Place a carton of ice cream behind some cereal boxes or puncture a can of motor oil and set it behind the cereal boxes.
- Rig egg cartons so a stack of them will topple over at a convenient time.
- Puncture a small hole in a gallon milk carton and let the fun flow.
- Slice the bottom of a box of dry laundry soap with a razor blade or utility knife.
- Hide a package of fish behind some canned goods near closing time.
- Cut the bottom of a few 10-ounce bags of potatoes and watch the fun when the spuds hit the decks.
- Place a dead rat in one of the bulk food containers.
- Mix some Kibbles 'n Bits in with the gorp in the bulk-food containers.
- Drop a small nest of maggots into some of the butcher's finest tenderloins.

SWEETHEARTS

- If your ex-husband refuses to pay child support, and he's abusive to you when you try to approach him about the subject, make up a poster that reads MY ABUSIVE EX-HUSBAND WON'T PAY HIS CHILD SUPPORT, and march in front of his place of business carrying the sign. Call a local TV station for good coverage and the police in the event he gets abusive again. It'll do wonders for his business reputation, if he owns the business. If not, his boss will likely have a few words to say to him about the unwanted attention he's brought to the establishment.
- If you want to make your former sweetie sweat a little, park you car in front of his

home for as long as the law will allow. Park it; take a cab or bus to work, to shop, or whatever; and then retrieve it before the towing or ticketing deadline. Do this repeatedly. He'll think he's being watched.

- Send off a hot response to one of those tabloid ads from "Foreign Girls Looking for American Husbands" in the name of your former sweetheart. The foreign recipient will get the hot letter, and she will go directly to your mark.

- If you still have access to your ex-lover/ aerobic instructor's apartment, get inside, find her aerobic togs, and smear the groin and chest areas of her leotard with crushed poison ivy. Later, when the exertion of her aerobic class opens her pores, she'll have a splendid outbreak in very sensitive areas.

SWIMMING POOLS

- Pour a gallon of motor oil in your mark's pool while he's away. He'll have to buy new filters, flush his lines and pump, and completely clean out the pool.
- Dump yellow dye in your victim's pool and send her an anonymous note saying you saw a large dog peeing in her pool.
- Add extract of toxicodendron (the nonvolatile oil found in the poison ivy plant) to your mark's swimming pool. He'll

be just itching to find out what happened.

- If you know that people of color have been treated badly or refused entry by community swimming pool employees, get hold of some orange dye marker solution used by Special Forces for air/sea rescue work and load up the lily white pool with it. It will not only ruin the pool full of water but will mess up the filters and pumps and coat the bottom and sides of the pool a vivid orange at the same time.

- If your target has drained his pool and will be having it refilled, get some straight pins, waterproof glue, and some paint that matches the inside of your target's pool. Paint the pins, let them dry, add glue, and stick them all over the shallow end of the pool—especially around the steps. Nice way to stick it to your barefoot mark.

- If your mark is overly boastful about having a pool, maybe he should be even closer to it. Using a long hose, jug, and funnel, create a siphon, placing one end of the hose in the pool, holding the other end above pool level and pouring water using the jug and funnel into the hose. Keep going until the air bubbles stop coming out the other end of the hose. When the water starts to flow, stick the other end of the hose through an open window in your target's game room or study. That'll give him something to spout off about.

TAILGATERS

- Rig up a switch connected to your brake lights and one to your reverse lights. When the driver behind you gets too close to your bumper, flip one of the switches. From behind, it will look like you're braking or, worse, backing up!
- Rig up an ultrapowerful spotlight to the roof rack or bumper of your car. When you have a nighttime tailgater, zap 'em with the light.

TAXIS

- Call every taxi service in town and send them to the victim's home 30 minutes apart all night. Ask that the drivers indicate their arrival by ringing her doorbell. If you do this often enough, she will never be able to get a taxi when she needs one.

TEACHERS

- If you've been handed an unfair grade by an insolent teacher who refuses to reconsider, get her to a library where they use an electronic sensor to catch people pilfering books. Go to the periodical section and remove several of the metallic sensor strips from some magazines. Locate your mark and, at an appropriate time, carefully plant the sensor strips on her books, briefcase, overcoat, purse, etc. Then stick around and enjoy the fun when she tries to go out the door. Your planted sensors will set off the bell and will cause extreme shock, upset, indignation, and confusion. With luck, only one sensor will be found at first, and the mark will try to leave again, only to set off the sensors once again.
- Make a small hole in the tip of a piece of chalk and fill it with a match head. Glue back some of the displaced chalk powder to cover it, but leave the very top exposed. As soon as that piece of chalk hits the blackboard, the teacher will see the light.

TELEPHONE ANSWERING MACHINES

- Call your mark's phone when you know she won't be there to answer it and don't say anything, just leave the phone off the hook long enough to use up the tape.
- Phone your target's answering machine repeatedly and fill the tape with static noise, vomiting sounds, the sound of a toilet flushing. Your target will have to listen to at least part of each message to ensure that there isn't an important one among them.
- If your target is married, get someone of the

opposite sex to leave a compromising message along the lines of: "Hi darling, I managed to get your phone number from your office. I don't know why you're being so secretive—we love each other, don't we? Call me today; I've got something really important to tell you. Love you."

- If your target is a family man, have a male accomplice call and leave this message: "Ah, Mr. Target. Sorry I've missed you, but our mutual friend is eager to see the pictures you mentioned. I've told him what a little beauty (name of target's child) is, and he can't wait to teach him some new games. I'm sure you understand. If the fee we discussed is a problem, I'm sure we can come to a new agreement, but please call me back soon. Thank you."

- If you have access to your target's home or business answering machine, substitute your own prerecorded message tape for your target's. Be creative with this.

TELEPHONES

- Any time you see a TV ad in which the announcer says: "Call this toll-free number now—operators are standing by!" Call and order the product in the victim's name.

- Every time you see a newspaper or magazine ad that allows you to order anything C.O.D. or "bill me later," do it in your victim's name. Try to order items that would be objectionable to him.

- Call your mark's spouse saying you're the desk clerk at the Happy Nights Inn and that he left an overcoat in the room when he was there the other night. Say that you got the home phone number from a business card in the coat pocket. Ask that she come pick up the coat.

- Call the victim's spouse, angrily accusing him of playing around with your spouse. If you know of exact times he has been away from home recently, list those as rendezvous times. Threaten violence if the affair isn't broken off immediately. Cry on the phone and talk about the children.

- When the victim's spouse is away from home, call him at work and in an excited voice tell him water is gushing out from under the front door of his home. Or tell him you saw smoke coming out a window. Or confide that you saw his wife and another man check into the No-Tell Motel.

- Make long-distance calls to massage parlors or dating and escort services. Tell the operator you want to bill the calls to your home phone and give her the victim's number. Talk as long as you can and ask the place to send any brochures it has to the victim's home.

- Whenever you're out of town, place a collect call to the victim's home. Have the operator say that it's his brother John or sister Jane calling (you'll have to know the right names). When he accepts the call, put down the phone and walk away.

- Posing as an emergency room clerk, call the victim at work and tell him his wife has been badly injured in a car accident and that he should rush right over. He'll probably be so upset that he'll rush to the hospital without first phoning home to check if it's true.

- When your mark goes on vacation, call the personnel department where she works and, using her name, say that you quit, that you've found a better job and won't be back.

- Call your mark in the middle of the night and ask for some fictitious person. Let's call him "Davey Jones." The mark will tell you there's no Davey Jones there, that you've reached a wrong number. Have several accomplices call the same number at 10-minute intervals, each asking to speak to Davey Jones. Finally, call back and say, "Hello (use the mark's first name), this is Davey Jones. Any calls for me?"

- When you get a call that's a wrong number, wait for a few moments of silent effect to build up just after you answer the phone, then laugh as hollowly and mockingly as you can right into the mouthpiece, and, without saying a word, hang up. Don't answer the phone if it rings again right away.

- Call about 200 people in hopes that at least 50 of them will not be home and will have an answering machine. Leave the message that they need to call (mark's name) back any time after midnight tonight and leave your mark's number. Indicate that it is very, very important or you wouldn't ask to be called so late.

- Unscrew the mouthpiece on your mark's telephone. Note the metallic contact on the bottom of that loose cylinder with the holes in the top. Spray that contact area with clear paint or coat it with clear nail polish. This will disrupt the electrical contact and disable the telephone.

- If your target relies on her telephone to do business, put her temporarily out of business by calling her from a public phone in an out-of-the-way place. As soon as she answers, walk away without hanging up the phone. She won't be able to use her phone until the calling end is hung up or until the telephone company has been called from another phone and can sort out the problem.

- Unplug your mark's phone and paint the contact with clear fingernail polish. Replace it in the socket and your target won't be able to reach out and touch anyone.

- Cut a couple of the wires on the circuit board of your mark's phone. When he punches the numbers, the associated digits will fail to register. You could also disconnect the bell on his phone so that incoming calls never get answered. He'll think he's been deserted. And maybe he should be.

- If your mark is one of those rude people who uses her mute button so she can make snide comments about her callers, find the mute button connection and cut it. All of a sudden your mark will become more open and honest with her callers.

- Apply a layer of the clear, instant self-tanning cream to the earpiece of your mark's telephone.

- Call in bomb threats from your mark's phone and then leave, making sure the phone is off the hook. It will be, but your mark won't.

- Phone your target's house when you know he won't be in but his parents will. When they say he's not in, ask to leave a message and say something to the effect that you paid for your dope and you're tired of waiting for it. Say you expect immediate delivery and, if your don't get it, there'll be hell to pay.

- Make a call to 911 from your hysterical target to the effect that he's taken poison, is going to blow up the neighborhood with a TNT bomb in his apartment, and will shoot anyone who comes looking for him. Authorities should be at his apartment shortly with a stomach pump, a straitjacket, and a jackhammer to tear down his walls.

- Call the neighborhood gossip in your mark's area and, identifying yourself as a news reporter, ask the gossip how long the mark has been running a brothel out of her house or whether, in the gossip's opinion, the mark seems like the type who would flash small children in the park.

97

TELEPHONE SOLICITORS

- Tired of telephone solicitors disturbing your dinner wanting to know if you'd like to buy their product? Keep an athletic whistle by the phone and next time they call, well, you know how to whistle, don't you? Just put your lips together and blow. This works well with harassing phone callers, too. Teach 'em to ask for a blow job over the phone.

- To ensure that a phone solicitor won't call back, listen to them for a while and then ask a series of questions, sounding more and more excited each time. After about five minutes, give a heavy moan, and scream, "Oh yes! Yes! I'm coming!" Then clear your throat and say, in your normal voice, "Thank you very much. That felt so good. Thank you."

- Find out the name and address of the company pestering you with phone calls as well as the name of the boss. Find out where he lives and use the phone directory to get his phone number. Phone him remorselessly at inopportune times. Offer lifetime memberships in pet-of-the-month clubs, try to sell him made-to-measure condoms, boots for his cat, anything. Call in the middle of the night and offer to sell him sleeping pills. Eventually your voice will become familiar to him. When he asks why you're doing this, tell him and demand to have your name taken off the company's list.

- Listen to the caller long enough to get the name and address of her company, and then hang up and write the company billing them for your time, inconvenience, and the use of your private line and equipment. Tell it that additional fees will be charged for any additional calls and to remit promptly to avoid legal action.

TELETHONS

- If your mark is especially interested in a particular telethon, and you know she'll be up watching the entire thing, call the telethon pledge number and, using her name, pledge $5,000 with an unusual conditional request. Tell the phone person that the pledge will be honored only if one of the guest celebrities acknowledges the pledge on the air with "my" (the mark's) name. If you can, join the mark for a beer while you watch the telethon together. When she hears her name and the amount of her pledge, she'll be in shock, while you pat her on the back and tell her what a fantastic thing it is she's done.

TELEVANGELISTS

- If you're a woman jogger and are verbally accosted by some street preacher calling you a "harlot and a whore," as you pass the street corner congregation, stop running, look him dead in the crotch, smile, and in your sexiest voice, say "Oh, and I've given you a hard-on, haven't I? I didn't know you even had one."

- If you know anyone who's wasted a lot of money on a televangelist's promise of a cure, borrow some hymnals from the studio/church and white out the hymn numbers. Then, using printed numbers, renumber about a third of the hymns. Nothing should match in any of the books. Return the hymnals in time for the next television taping, which will have to be stopped because of the musical chaos.

- When they pass the collection plate in these Church of the Charlatan chapters, contribute several coin-pack condoms individually wrapped in heavy gold foil.

THEFT

- Use No. 14 washers in newspaper vending machines, remove all the newspapers, and take them into bars or onto street corners and sell them yourself.
- If you suspect a neighbor is stealing wood from your winter supply, drill out a couple of pieces and put a quarter-ounce of black powder into the holes. Leave those logs on top, wait, and listen to hear which of your neighbors has a minor explosion!
- If you're tired of someone stealing your morning paper, get up early, dose the funnies and sports section with poison-oak extract, and leave it there for the thief. They'll be itchin' to read the news.
- If you're a mechanic and you have trouble with tool thieves, mix DMSO with croton oil and apply it to items in your shop most likely to be stolen. DMSO absorbs into the skin and carries the croton oil with it. Your thief will be so busy stealing away to tool the brown out of his briefs he'll forget about stealing your tools.

TOILETS

- Saturate some large, dry sponges with a thick starch solution. Squeeze them tightly into balls and tie them down as tightly as possible with tough string. Allow them to dry thoroughly and then remove the string; they will stay in their compressed state. Drop them into targeted toilets, flush, and walk away. The starch will dissolve, and the sponges will expand in the drainage system, causing disgusting backups.
- Liberally apply some extract of toxicodendron (poison ivy) to the toilet paper in your mark's bathroom.

- Stretch and place Saran Wrap very tightly across the top of the commode bowl so no creases show and then lower the seat gently in order to keep the trap in place. A piece of Plexiglas cut to fit the bowl dimensions exactly works nicely for this too.
- Paint a liberal coat of high-gloss enamel on your mark's toilet seat and forget to put up a "Wet Paint" sign.
- Turn off the water supply to your mark's toilet and flush it twice to empty the bowl. Then dump a load of freshly mixed concrete down it. Expanding insulation foam will also do the trick nicely.
- If your target has a septic tank, dump household bleach down it to destroy the bacteria needed to break down the waste. The tank will stop working and will have to be pumped out. Or dump a pound of dry yeast into the tank. The yeast will grow quickly and give off odoriferous gases that will back up in the pipes and waft through your target's home.

TOWING SERVICE

- Call a towing service and have the victim's car towed to a garage for a tuneup or paint job. Give a fictitious name so he'll have a tough time tracking down his auto.
- If your mark has a designated parking spot, go to a junkyard and buy a newly crushed wreck and arrange to have it towed to your target's normal parking spot. Coordinate the time the wreck is delivered with your moving your mark's car a couple of parking places away.
- Get your hands on an uncrushed wreck that is similar to your mark's car and coordinate moving your mark's car with the delivery of the wreck to your mark's assigned parking space. Pour a little gasoline over the wreck, toss a match, and disappear fast.

TRAVEL

- Make reservations for two in the victim's name at a high-class motel out of town. Give his home phone number and request confirmation two days before the reservation date.
- Book trips for two at a travel agency in your mark's name. Instead of giving his wife's name, list his secretary's or another woman's name. Have the itinerary mailed to his home.
- Apply for travel visas in your mark's name at the Washington, D.C., embassies of communist countries. Explain that you're interested in emigrating there because you're sick of the oppression in America. Have the visa information sent to the victim's place of employment.

LA TURISTA

- If your mark is traveling into Mexico or some other South or Central American country or even into Canada, report your suspicions to the authorities that she is a drug dealer. If you can, sneak some drugs into the mark's car, luggage, or person prior to her hitting a border point.

TV SETS

- Get several small magnets and place them on the screens of many of the TV sets on display in your target store. The magnets will attract particles from the electron guns of the TV receiver to that one spot and burn a "hole" in the tube.
- Take a large hand-held tape eraser and run it over the back of the color tube of your mark's television set. This will mess up the color alignment and could injure the line scan, too, if you're lucky.

TYPEWRITERS

- If your mark is a typist and uses a typewriter that has interchangeable balls, cover the balls heavily with either clear nail polish or a clear spray paint. The mark will type till his fingers fall off, but nothing will appear on the page.

URINE

- If you're tired of your neighbor's cats or dogs marking your territory as their own, drink some beer, eat some asparagus (to create a truly distinctive aroma), and collect your own urine sample. Put it into a spray bottle and mark your mark's property as soon as an opportunity presents itself. As a bonus, your mark's animals will try to reclaim their own territory with fresh sprays of their own. Remarkable . . .
- Freeze your urine into oversized cubes, which you can use to bombard your mark's redwood deck, flowers, garden, and so forth. The sun melts the ice, and the uric acid will do the rest.
- If you know of some low-lifes from a neighborhood nuisance bar that come outside and pee in the alley, get a trusted electrician friend to wire a 220-volt steel plate on the ground where they pee. It'll literally zap the piss right out of 'em.
- If your privacy is invaded by a company official who insists you take a urine test, substitute Diet Mountain Dew for your sample. This soft drink has the same pH and density as urine.

VD

- Call your city's VD hot line and say you caught your syphilis from the victim. The health department will send an investigator to quiz him about his sexual contacts.

VACATION RESORTS

- If you've been taken for a ride by the sharks at one of those beach holiday resorts, modify a radio-controlled model boat to carry a realistic model of a shark's fin. Glue the receiving antenna along the fin and then launch it wherever you want to create havoc among other resort guests.

VENDING MACHINES

- If you've ever been ripped off by a vending machine (and who among us hasn't?), wrap a wire around a big wad of cotton and stuff it up the coin return shaft in the offending machine until the wire is just above the opening and can't be seen. The next day, come back, pull out the wire and receive a refund of the fullest kind, you might say, with interest.

- Use brass washers in newspaper vending machines, or if you don't have any, there is usually a small hole on the tops of these machines. Stick a pin or something thin, strong, and sharp in there, push down, and pull on the door. It should open, and you'll have your paper.

VIDEOS

- Dub the soundtrack of some porn flick over your mark's nice home/family tapes.
- If you've ever been charged an overdue fine from a video rental store even though you returned the video on time, get an empty video box from the shop, place two large magnets in it, and superglue it shut. Drop the little magnetic bomb into the drop box just after the target store closes for a holiday, so that two days will elapse between damage and discovery.

VIP

- You know the type. That always unavailable VIP who could solve your problem on the phone if he weren't always tied up or in a meeting or just stepped out of the office. Next time, come armed with the name of the company CEO and, when you're again told Mr. VIP is unavailable, say that you thought (use VIP's name) could handle this situation, but since that doesn't seem to be the case and you'll be having lunch with the CEO (use his name here) soon anyway, you will just have to ask him to take care of the matter then.

VOMIT

- Vomit into Ziploc freezer bags that have been marked as stew, then store them in your mark's freezer.

WATER WELLS

- If your target lives outside of the municipal water area and has a well, you can put any number of additives in the water: roadkill, bleach, or dyes to name a few. You could also gorge yourself with greasy food like pizza and french fries, drink a lot of beer, and then go to your mark's water well, stick your finger down your throat, wiggle it a little, and vomit down the well. Wretch a pail of water, so to speak.

WEDDINGS

- Pose as a catering service and make arrangements to cater your mark's wedding reception.
- Find out who is catering your mark's wedding reception and call the company, posing as your distraught mark. Say something unexpected came up and you'll have to cancel your wedding plans.

WESTERN UNION

- Call the victim on his birthday saying you're from Western Union and have a moneygram

for him from his Aunt ____ in ____. Tell him he'll have to come by the office and pick it up. Tape the rapid chattering of your typewriter and the sound of its bell and play the tape during your call to simulate the sounds of a Western Union office.

WILLS

- Write your least favorite friend or relative into your last will and testament, bequeathing to them all your yachts, gold bullion, foreign holdings, and other valuable items you never had. In this way she will be shamed in front of others when the will is read.

WORK

- If your target is in a profession where he relies heavily on phone contacts, get his address/phone book, or rolodex and, using the same color ink, carefully alter a few digits in all the telephone numbers. Stick to those that can be easily changed—3 to an 8, 1 to a 4 or 7, and so on.
- If your target is one of those super-neat-desk freaks who is constantly rearranging the items on his desk in order of their size, superglue his pencil sharpener, in/out box, and stapler to the top of his desk.
- If it's your place of employ that you want to cause a little trouble for, place an ad in the newspaper for them, advertising for an "attractive female secretary, aged 18-25, white applicants preferred."
- If your company uses ceiling fans in the summer in its boardrooms, balance a couple of small bottles of opened ink on the still fan blades, near the center axis, just prior to an important meeting.

WRONG NUMBERS

- Next time you get a wrong number, don't just say they've reached a wrong number and hang up. Wait a couple of seconds, then, with a slight catch in your throat, whisper, "Oh, God, you don't know. (Whomever they asked for) has just died. I'm a neighbor, and we're all in shock. She's gone (sob). Please don't call here again." Then hang up.

XMAS

- Two weeks before Christmas, fill out a change of address card in your victim's name and mail it to the local post office. List the address of a local Salvation Army branch as his new address. Then call the Salvation Army, give the victim's name, and report that you're having your Christmas gifts routed to it this year.
- Discreetly leave a totally inappropriate Christmas present for the boss "from" your target.
- Wrap some especially grizzly roadkill in some festive Christmas paper and set it under your mark's tree.
- The way to deal with snooty, pushy shops or clerks who pressure you during the holiday buying season is to buy most everything they suggest, even going into extravagant upgrades in gift selection. Put all of this on plastic, so the snooty clerk/mark gets "credit" for the sale. Then do your real shopping and a few days later, calmly return your purchases to the snooty/pushy store for credit, saying, "After the intense sales pressure from (mark's name) wore off, I found I really didn't need any of this. So sorry."

ZIPPERS

- If you have to put up with some schmuck who is annoying and who also happens to wear a coat with a zipper, take a pair of pliers and firmly bend the right hand receiver (on men's coats—reverse for women's) just enough so the guide on the other side will not slip into the receiver. Don't leave plier marks or bend it so much that is is noticeable, just enough so it won't work. For your viewing pleasure, stand around and talk to your mark while he is trying to get this zapped zipper to work. It makes things more frustrating, especially if you're putting on subtle pressure or acting semi-impatient.